We Are Tottenham

To Cath and Daniel

To Jo, Ellen and Carla, and Dad,
who brought me up the Spurs Way

WE ARE TOTTENHAM

Voices from White Hart Lane

Martin Cloake and **Adam Powley**

MAINSTREAM
PUBLISHING

EDINBURGH AND LONDON

First published in Great Britain in 2004 by
MAINSTREAM PUBLISHING COMPANY (EDINBURGH) LTD
7 Albany Street
Edinburgh EH1 3UG

ISBN 1 84018 831 6

A catalogue record for this book is available from the British Library

Typeset in Frutiger and Janson
Printed and bound in Great Britain by
Antony Rowe Ltd, Chippenham, Wiltshire

Contents

Acknowledgements

This book was inspired by many conversations with many Spurs fans over the years, but in particular by the enthusiastic storytelling of Bruce Lee and a long interview with Norman Jay for the now defunct Tottenham fanzine *Off the Shelf*. Years of travelling with and supporting Spurs have also provided much inspiration, and we'd like to thank all those people who, over the years, have made following our club such a rewarding experience.

Thanks to all our interviewees for giving up their time and sharing their views, stories and their passion for the club – it is this that makes the book what it is. Jim Duggan deserves special thanks for being an invaluable source of information and leads. Thanks also to Chris Kaufman for his help, to Steve Davies and Melissa Oliveck, and to Jim Brigden, Fulham Fred, Annelise Jespersen, Julian Richards and the Bricklayers crew for enriching the matchday experience.

Derek Ridgers has put in much time and effort on the pictures side, along with Mark Leech and Ed Griffin at Offside Photography. Thanks, too, to Noleen Lance, Simon Battle and Cath MacKenzie. Tanya Smale, Rob and Mary Haynes and Jo Powley performed sterling work in helping us transcribe the interviews. Bernie Kingsley has always been prepared to assist with the 1,001 questions we've had and, similarly, thank you to Pete Panayi for his valuable advice. Andy Lyons and Doug Cheeseman at *When Saturday Comes*, Andrew Shields at *Time Out*, Alex Fynn and H. Davidson have also provided much needed and much appreciated guidance. Thanks should also be extended to all on the *Sunday Mirror* sports desk and the boys of *FTT* (as was) and to Hunter Davies for his inspirational *The Glory Game*.

Thanks to all at Mainstream, especially Bill Campbell for having faith in the book, Graeme Blaikie for steering it through the editorial process and to Lizzie Cameron in design.

And a huge thanks to our families, not only for putting up with us while writing the book, but also for their many years of sufferance in having husbands, dads and sons who support Spurs.

We would also like to pay tribute to Fred Dowry. He had only missed a few first-team games in over 30 years, and had an incredible record of not having missed a single first-team game, friendlies and all, since autumn 1990. Fred had agreed to be interviewed for this book but, ironically, the demands on his time that his dedication to Spurs and his work as a manager for BT involved meant that arranging a meeting wasn't easy, and we were still attempting to set something up when, on 25 January 2004, Fred died on his way to Manchester for his team's FA Cup fourth-round tie. Fred was not only loyal but, according to the many individuals who urged us to interview him, thoughtful and knowledgeable, and his presence is not only greatly missed in these pages, but among the large group of fans who had the pleasure of his company on matchdays. Fred showed what football means to people.

Foreword

I always thought I was alone in the way I follow football, loving a team while hating them, cheering while moaning, admiring while despising, madly optimistic on one day, one game, even during one movement when miraculously three passes get put together, while at the same time feeling deeply cynical and pessimistic and depressed.

Now I know, having read this fascinating book, that I am totally boringly normal. It turns out many football fans are like this. And with Spurs, it's what *most* of them are like all the time, have been perhaps for the last 30 years since we last had anything decent to get excited and hopeful about.

I say 'we' because I am a Spurs fan, but one of the strengths of this book is that it applies to so many fans, here, there and everywhere. We have all been there, saw it, felt it, vowed never to go again, said we'd make sure that lousy club never gets another penny of our money, till, of course, next Saturday at three o'clock. 'Next Saturday at Three O'clock' is, of course, a generic term, with little relation to modern reality, referring to something that no longer exists, as quaint as the use of 'Fleet Street' to describe the national press when none of them are based in Fleet Street any more.

What Martin Cloake and Adam Powley have done is talk to a cross section of a dozen or so Spurs fans, from the age of seven to eighty-five, men and women, black and white, Jews and gentiles, mostly north Londoners, but others who travel from as far away as Carlisle and Scandinavia. There is even an Arsenal fan, Tom Watt, who has some very sensible things to say, for an Arsenal fan, about the present state of Spurs. I love the DJ, unknown to me until I read this book but apparently world famous, who did the music for Thierry Henry's wedding, during which he wore a little cockerel badge.

We Are Tottenham

Moaning about the present state of Spurs, that's a recurring theme for all of them. Remembering the glory days gone by, that's another constant element, even from those too young to have ever seen the Double team. But, of course, fans have always moaned. In a book I did about Spurs, *The Glory Game*, in 1972, there were lots of moaners amongst the supporters, hating the fuddy-duddy board, thinking Martin Chivers didn't try hard enough. I remember one wealthy fan so worried and nervous about the team that he never saw the end of any match, unable to take the disappointment which he always expected.

There is today a great dislike of the way the club has been run these last couple of decades, as if more interested in merchandising and sponsorship than the ordinary fans. Football fans generally feel this.

One of the many personal hatreds is the list of box owners they insist on printing in the programme, as if we care, as if we want to know their lousy names, most of them anyway companies using shareholders' money for their corporate entertaining. I always tear out those pages in the programme, effing and blinding, which is self-defeating, as I collect Spurs programmes, have them going back to 1909. I also collect handbooks, photos, books, anything really to do with Spurs, as I love them so dearly, always have done, always will, the bastards.

I'll keep this book safe as well. It's the sort of record all clubs should have, of what fans thought and felt at a particular moment in time, the sort of voices you normally don't hear and certainly directors and owners never seem to hear, stuck in their plc towers, isolated in a world of sponsors and merchandisers.

One nice idea, suggested by one of the fans interviewed in this book – one of the hooligan element – is that fans who have had a season ticket for ten years should have the next year free. Players get testimonials, even when they are already millionaires, and we all foolishly go along and pay them even more money, so why shouldn't fans get a little perk now and again for loyalty and devotion? No chance, of course. Our duty is to hand over small fortunes to our chosen club, blindly and loyally support, know and keep in our place, and if we moan, do it quietly, please, over there, don't get in the way of the corporate guests.

We all know that big clubs don't give a bugger about the loyalty of their fans. Here, at last, some fans answer back, even though they could all well be talking amongst themselves, amongst ourselves. Most fans will at least recognise themselves somewhere in this book.

Hunter Davies

Introduction

There's no logic to it. Fans choose to support a football team in spite of, rather than because of, any rational analysis. We don't switch that support to the latest successful team, and we appear as attached to the defeats as we are to the – usually more infrequent – successes. It's probably because of this that we often go to ridiculous lengths to prove our loyalty and feel so strongly about the team we support. It's almost as if we have to cover for the fact that our passion is based upon such shaky foundations by the intensity of our support.

Most fans used to look forward to a season with hopes of success, maybe even winning something. Now, fewer fans than ever harbour realistic hopes of winning trophies, and success is increasingly defined as not failing as badly as most others. The game is not entirely predictable – in recent years Wycombe Wanderers' cup run, Ipswich beating Internazionale and Greece winning Euro 2004 have all defied predictions to keep some of the old magic alive. But most fans know that being there or thereabouts is as much as we can hope for.

So what makes most football fans put so much into backing a hopeless cause? Why, when we know we won't, or can't, be the best, do we continue to hope that we might be? Maybe it's just because football supporters defy all logic that supporting a team is so popular; maybe there are as many reasons as there are fans?

What is interesting about much of what has been written about football fans is that we are still seen more as a crowd than as the individuals who make up that crowd. When the whistle sounds for kick-off, the bank manager and the grafter, the old lady who's been going for years and the kids at their first live game, the ageing lads and the family groups, all come together for the only time in their otherwise separate existences in wanting their team to succeed. This unity of purpose has led many in the game's administration, and in the ranks of the growing network of supporter organisations, to make the mistake of assuming that unity exists outside of a desire to see the team succeed. Everyone wants to win, but ask how it should be done and the unity breaks down; the individuals in the crowd assert themselves once more.

This book is an attempt to bring those individuals to the fore in order to give a more accurate picture of the personality of a crowd at one particular club, Tottenham Hotspur. We chose this club for the nakedly partisan reason that we are both Spurs fans. But Spurs also provide an interesting subject because of the club's peculiar history.

For years, Spurs were big-spending, big-name heavyweights, a fashionable London club with a fine pedigree and a history of groundbreaking success at home and in Europe. The authors' generation of thirtysomething supporters grew up secure in the belief that we were one of the so-called big-five clubs which dominated English football, but the truth is that since the 1970s Spurs have never been one of the elite. There have been fits and starts, but achievements have not been built upon and promise has remained largely unfulfilled. To make matters even more frustrating for Spurs fans, the club has laid the foundations upon which others have built success. After becoming the first club to float on the Stock Exchange, Tottenham Hotspur fumbled and bungled while others forged ahead to take advantage of the most affluent period in English football history. The first British club to win a European trophy now looks enviously towards even the minor European club competitions, and Manchester United have become the biggest commercial brand in world football thanks to a marketing manager who learned his trade at Spurs before being pushed out.

What could be the defining moment of Spurs' recent history was captured by the original Tottenham fanzine *The Spur* just after Gary Lineker signed for the club. Pictured shaking hands with then manager Terry Venables, Lineker sprouts a speech bubble saying, 'I'm really looking forward to playing alongside Chris Waddle, boss,' while Venables is saying, 'Er, there's something I've been meaning to tell you . . .' Waddle, of course, had been sold that very same summer. 'Almost, but not quite, there' could replace 'To dare is to do' as the club motto, although more recently 'No chance of ever getting there' has seemed more accurate.

The toll on Spurs fans has been heavy. Always a demanding crowd, the spiral of decline has led to division and ill feeling. Some fans seem unable to come to terms with the fact that Spurs do not have a divine right to be big and successful, while others – particularly younger fans – are fed up with the constant comparisons with times past. As football fans became more organised – another development which Spurs supporters helped to pioneer – so supporter politics at Spurs descended into insular, bitter splintering.

But what's remarkable about Tottenham fans is that the numbers have not fallen away. For a group of people so often labelled fickle, they have shown remarkable loyalty. If this is what happens while the club is underachieving, consider what could happen if success finally does come – a thought that can't be very far from the minds of the investment company executives who currently own the club.

So who are these Tottenham fans, these fickle but loyal, generous but mean-spirited, unreasonable but patient people? While the accusation 'typical Spurs fan' may conjure up the image of the strutting and cocksure creature on the club badge, flash southern softies, or any of the traits mentioned above, the truth is there's no such thing as a typical fan of any club. A crowd is dehumanised if it is shorn of its individual identities, and we saw what that can lead to at Hillsborough, where 96 people lost their lives because they were part of a football crowd. If police and stewards had listened to the individual voices of those in the Hillsborough crowd rather than viewed it as a single, threatening entity that needed to be controlled, maybe tragedy could have been avoided.

For the purposes of this book, we have tried to interview a cross-section of fans, and to weave their stories in with the story of one season at the club. We do not pretend that this is a definitive profile, more a glimpse of the diversity that makes up the club's support – both at the grounds and away from them. Neither do we pretend that this diversity of support is peculiar to Spurs.

What we deliberately set out to challenge was the way fans are often represented in the mass media, now that it has finally discovered we exist. It is still a relatively new development that sees fans consulted by those who cover the game, or even that we are seen as part of football's constituency. But it's as if we have to conform to some predetermined image. If we are not hooligans, we are fanatics, the sort of people who will either proclaim our willingness to watch our team rather than have sex, or at least make sure we're wearing a team bobble hat while we are in the act.

One of the fascinating things about reading these contributions is realising how so many different people can come together as one so regularly. There is also a wealth of vivid images and a lot of fun. Spurs fans will enjoy sharing the experiences, but we hope many more people will be able to draw something from it. And if this book goes some way towards giving those faces in the crowd an identity, that would be something of a result.

Once, while driving to a game, someone said to one of the authors, 'I wish Spurs would win the League so I could stop going to see them.' It's a remark that has stuck with us – perhaps because we are part of a generation of Spurs fans who have seen the club slide from major player to also-ran. Now, there is a constant fear that if we give up on what we think will probably be another season of underachievement, our team will sweep the board and all those years of suffering will have been in vain.

That is typical of the tortured, perverse relationship fans have with their clubs, but it also emphasises one important point. As much as the game in its current bloated, preening, cash-rich incarnation may like to pretend the fans who pay to watch matches are just minor players in the modern business of football, the fact is that the passion and dedication of fans to their club still provides the engine that powers the football juggernaut. Football without the fans just would not work, so it is not for nothing that even at the underachieving, bungling, corporate new Spurs, the fans still sing, 'We are Tottenham.'

1

Super Tottenham, from the Lane: Bruce Lee

We are Tottenham,
We are Tottenham,
Super Tottenham,
From the Lane

When your name's Bruce Lee and you're growing up in north London, you need a quick wit. 'You'll never believe the amount of Hi-Karate aftershave I used to get for Christmas and birthdays,' says Bruce, a 39-year-old tax consultant who lives in Enfield. He'd be the first to argue that a sense of humour is also required for one of his greatest passions – supporting Tottenham Hotspur.

Humour is probably what helps Bruce maintain the optimism for which he is known and liked by the extended group of Spurs fans he's been watching matches with for years. But as the 2003–04 season began, he admitted to finding his usual optimism hard to maintain.

The phrase 'Tottenham through-and-through' certainly applies to Bruce, and he'll admit that his life has been shaped by Spurs. 'I left school when I was 15 and left, if I'm honest, because of football,' he says. But although he readily confesses to his obsession, he's no one-dimensional fanatic. He's almost as passionate about music as he is about Spurs, and his awareness of a wider world beyond football allows him a sense of perspective that often seems to be missing when football people talk.

Most of all, Bruce likes to talk, and for those who accompany him to matches, the tales he spins are as much a part of the entertainment of a day at the football as the game itself. He's got a rich vein of experiences to draw from, such as one incident from the late 1970s. 'We used to go on the private coaches. We went to Norwich once, and the coachload we were with turned over a sweet stall outside Harlow station. The police were called, and we got pulled up further along the A11. I think they just followed the trail of lemonade bottles.

'The coach was full of kids, and some of the older blokes were cramming bars of chocolate and bags of crisps in their mouths and shouting, "Eat the evidence!" We all got taken to Harlow nick, and my little brother Andrew was with me. He could only have been about eight or nine, but he was a cunning little sod. They held us on the coach waiting for the ringleaders to own up, and my little brother looked at me at one point and said, "This is silly, we're going to be here all night," and he started crying.

'Within two minutes, some policewoman got us off this coach. I think it was when Andrew was getting off that he said, "I would have liked to watch this." I mean, he'd eaten two dozen Mars bars himself!'

Bruce first became aware of Spurs around 1972. 'I lived about half a mile from the ground. There was no parental influence, no one else in the family interested. I was aged about six or seven and just suddenly got into it, kicking a ball around with all the local kids. Spurs were the local team; everyone was a Spurs fan. It was quite rare living in Tottenham and being an Arsenal fan. In fact, in those days it was getting towards the period when it was unhealthy to be an Arsenal fan in that area.

'We played just near Bruce Castle Park. My first memory was saying, "Can we look after your car, Mister?" to the fans turning up for games. Our estate overlooked the Tottenham end of the Roundway, and we used to sit down there. You could hear the ground across Bruce Castle Park. So, when a friend of the family said they'd take me along there, I jumped at it. It was a Spurs v. Man United game; Martin Chivers scored for us.'

Once the die was cast there was no looking back, and Bruce soon started taking his little brother to White Hart Lane. They were formative years. 'I look back at some of the games I went to and, I say this to my mother now, I can't believe the things she used to let me do. I think because my mum and dad split up I was not necessarily streetwise, but I was quite mature for a boy of my age. I would have only been about eight myself when I first started going, so there must have been a limit to my mother's patience, or wallet, or whatever. But I went a couple of times a season for a few years.

'But my mother is eternally grateful to Tottenham to be honest. Although it got me in scrapes, I think it kept me on the straight and narrow. Once I'd been, it became all-pervasive very quickly.'

By the mid-1970s, going to a football match could be a risky business. 'I went to that Chelsea game, I think it was '73–'74, when there was a famous punch-up on the pitch because both teams were dreadful then. Spurs actually managed to beat Chelsea and it was more or less a knockout blow about five or six games before the end of the season. Alfie Conn took the mickey out of them. The game kicked off about 20 minutes late because there was fighting, and I watched the game from an aisle on the Shelf. Supposedly, there were about 55,000 in there.

'At that game, a fella on our estate got turned in to the police by his old dear, because there was a big ruck on the pitch before the game – all these blokes in loon pants with scarves tied round their waists kicking seven bells out of each other. It was on the evening news. One of them was this kid on our estate, and his mum apparently took him down by the ear hole to Tottenham nick.'

The growing culture of violence at football matches worried many parents, and Bruce found his match-going curtailed. 'The most obvious example was Millwall in '77 when all the stuff about Harry the Dog had been on *Panorama*. There was a lot of talk about what Millwall were going to do to Tottenham, and we played them on Boxing Day. By all accounts it was fairly fearsome. It was an 11.30 kick-off, and I really wanted to be there, but my mum put her foot down on that occasion.

'Up until that point I was taking my little brother with me, who was three or four years younger, and she trusted me not to get involved. There was the isolated occasion where she would firmly say, "You're not going", but other than that I don't know whether she really thought about it. I don't think she realised it was quite as rough as it was, but I look back and even though I take the piss a bit, I do thank her because I grew up quick. I just saw things and got grounded fairly early on.'

Away games are a whole new adventure, and regular travelling to see Tottenham play away soon became a real draw for ten-year-old Bruce. 'The first couple of times I was chaperoned by another friend of the family. I don't think he ever came to White Hart Lane with me, but he would have been late teens, early 20s, and we went to away games on Grey Green coaches. They used to drop you outside the Co-op in Tottenham High Road and pick you up.

'Burnley was an eye-opener. Even at that age I knew the Hovis adverts were a stereotype, but Burnley did look like that. I'm not playing the sophisticated Londoner, because Tottenham's always been fairly unsophisticated. Maybe some children are always off to Cannes and Hollywood; I got to go to Burnley and Norwich.'

But for a kid from Tottenham, those trips were every bit as exotic. 'There was a period when the home games became very run of the mill; you were looking forward to the away trips. It was great going to a new ground that you'd seen from a certain angle on the television and then you're there and it's all fresh.

'You used to read about all these long-haired layabouts banging on the coach windows singing, "Tottenham boys we are here." I remember people jumping up and down and singing and hollering and seeing these locals looking up; it was an amazing feeling. It wasn't that you wanted to make them think, "Oh, my God, lock up your daughters." It was a sort of expression of pride about where you were from. It was strangely liberating at the time.'

Once a kid develops a strong enough interest in something, the family usually fall in with it. Bruce's proved to be no exception. 'My dad used to work for Tottenham bus garage, and for a while after we'd moved out to Buckhurst Hill I carried on going to school in Tottenham. He used to run me down to Tommy Moore's school on the bus. Sometimes he used to take his bus out during the day and I used to say, "Go and pick us up a couple of tickets." He'd do it, even though he didn't know the first thing about football.

'Then we started going with the supporters' club coaches. They were quite maternal, the old dears who used to run it.'

Supporters' clubs at this time were not the bodies that have become identified as the voice of football fans. They were essentially travel clubs run by slightly older, respectable types who wouldn't have dreamt of passing comment on how the club was run. Bruce began to use the coaches and trains organised by the Spurs Supporters' Club, whose distinctive oval badges are still a prized possession today.

He has also made trips abroad. For football fans, particularly English ones, it's a fact of life that reputations precede them, and

Bruce has seen the best and worst of English club fans overseas while following Spurs in Europe. Spurs fans have a chequered record on the Continent, although there can't have been many trips like Bruce's first European experience.

'It would have been about '78–'79, I guess. Spurs played a friendly against PSV Eindhoven. A mate of mine saw it advertised in the local paper, and coaches were leaving from Harlow. This game wasn't even in Eindhoven; it was somewhere called Beilen or somewhere, some small non-league town.

'The ground had temporary stands all around it and there were loads of boisterous Spurs fans there, but no real misbehaviour. This fella that I booked with, his older brother was a nutter, one of the main boys, and he lived out our way. I knew he was going on a different coach and that they'd run into loads of trouble in Amsterdam. But we ended up going straight to this place, and it was just fantastic. You start to feel so grown up when you get out there: it wasn't because we were into any trouble or anything; it was just hilarious. You could just wander on to the pitch and there was a 50-a-side match going on at half-time. As we left the town on the coaches, the locals were out on their front lawns waving.'

Bruce's appetite was whetted, and the growing success of Keith Burkinshaw's early 1980s side meant that soon the team were back in Europe proper.

'The first competitive one I went to was Ajax in '81 after we won the Cup, which was the first game back after we'd been banned. There was trouble there. I remember Stevie Perryman on the pitch beforehand telling everyone, "Let's not get us thrown out again, it's taken us this long to get back."

'But for the same reasons that five or six years before Burnley had been such a treat, Amsterdam was special. I went on the organised Spurs tours in Europe, although I shunned that at home. So it wasn't really a question of carousing – you weren't given any chance – it was just going somewhere different and seeing the different fans and the different faces.

'We had a good side in those days, so after that I went to a few. We went to Frankfurt in 1982, which was an experience. We got off these coaches in Frankfurt and there were these German policemen, very militaristic in their stance – 7 ft 3 in. tall, refugees from a sci-fi movie, all in combat gear – stood there passively looking at us as we got off.

We Are Tottenham

'By the end of the night, Spurs had lost but got through, I think, so people should have been in good spirits. I remember thinking there's not going to be trouble here because everyone's seen that these policemen are armed to the teeth. But there were people climbing over the gates and going toe-to-toe with these blokes in visors and helmets. In the end, the German police didn't know what to do and they opened the gates. I don't know if it was widespread trouble that day, but it was almost like they were prepared to test the limits. It was unfortunate because I think that sort of mentality lasted for long, long after it should have done.'

Unfortunately, it wasn't long before events off the pitch were once again to overshadow what the team did on it. In the 1983–84 season, Tottenham's successful UEFA Cup run was accompanied by ugly scenes in Rotterdam for the match against Feyenoord and in Brussels for the first leg of the final against Anderlecht. Tottenham fans were labelled 'the shame of Britain', but many, like Bruce, had gone for the football and the experience, and they were appalled at the scenes they witnessed. He takes up the tale of the Rotterdam trip.

'I've never seen so many Spurs fans in a place. At a game like that in an English city they don't allow you to congregate in such numbers at football matches. If you're there two or three hours before kick-off, then that's extreme. It was the era when people were going around thieving, and we'd be standing outside the pub and somebody would come and try and sell you a Lacoste T-shirt still in its cellophane.

'We got into this ground and there was lots of history between Spurs and Feyenoord. Stupidly, some Spurs fans had bought tickets to cause trouble in the other end. Even by that stage, it was just about past the era of taking the other end and widespread disturbance inside football grounds. So it was quite weird: we were sat there about ten minutes before kick-off and at the opposite end the crowd parted and this mob of Spurs fans had gone steaming down the middle of the terrace and this big hole appeared. There had been a good atmosphere and all of a sudden it all closed around them and you could see people thrown out, covered in blood.

'Coming outside that ground was just horrific. You could see people coming back down talking about Dutch fans with knives. I had two programmes, one I bought for someone else and I had one for myself, so I adjusted them under my clothing and I thought, "If anyone comes at me with a knife, they're going to get the programme first." But there were people openly brandishing knives, you don't often see that, really, even going to as many football matches as I have: openly brandishing knives. Spurs fans, to be honest, were being ill behaved. We heard there were people that were thrown off motorway bridges and all sorts.

'We had a tendency to think of the Dutch as all very friendly and smoking spliffs and wearing clogs and wanting to speak English better than you and knowing all about Port Vale reserves. I think they just proved that night that a proportion of their population is the same as ours; they were rabid, looking out for English fans.

'We were supposed to stay the night in Rotterdam, and a few friends and I squeezed on to the train and I said, "Look, I'm not getting off at the main station, I'm going straight home," and about two or three of us did.'

When Spurs arrived in Brussels for the final, the fear some of their supporters had spread in previous rounds led to a tragic incident, as a jumpy barman fired a shotgun into a crowded bar and killed a young Tottenham fan from Wood Green. Bruce remembers it well.

'It should have been one of the high points, but a Spurs fan got shot dead in a bar round the corner from the hotel we were staying in. A friend of mine was in the bar. In the morning, people were apologising to us and we didn't know what they were apologising for until we heard what had happened.

'That was the night before the game, so on the evening of the game itself there was a real atmosphere. After the game, we were caught up in the aftermath because we came out of the ground late and we were wandering around – we lost some people and we were wondering what the easiest way to get back into town to our hotel was. We happened to be behind a mob of Spurs fans who were taking some vengeance for the night before. There were bars turned over and cars on fire. We got out of it pretty quick.'

Things had gone so far that even committed fans like Bruce gave up on travelling abroad for a while. 'It really did put me off and I stopped going,' he admits. 'I also met my wife around about that time and then there was Heysel, so there wouldn't have been any English competition anyway.'

Despite the bad experiences, Bruce has never lost his affection for the Spurs crowd. He is philosophical about the criticism thrown their way. 'If we're disliked it's because we're seen as big-time Charlies with no reason to be swaggering. Obviously there's an element of truth in that.'

But, in common with many Spurs fans, it's the 'f' word that really gets him going. 'One of the things I get a bee in my bonnet about is Spurs fans being called fickle. I think there's plenty of adjectives you could apply, but I don't think fickle is one of them. Fickle to me always meant the opposite of loyal, and I think that Spurs fans are as loyal as ever, perhaps slightly above the Premiership average. We're quick to jump down the players' throats as a crowd, but I would still stick the loyalty tag on us because I think we've had an awful lot of gruel over the last ten years. We're always hanging on for a better day, and I think the crowd has held up reasonably well.'

In the end, maybe it just comes down to believing in your own, and Bruce is clear about the greater scheme of things. 'When the old genius Peter Cook was on the telly, I used to say you can't tell me that the fact that he's so funny isn't down to the fact that he's a Spurs fan. Jeremy Beadle's Arsenal, Peter Cook's Spurs.'

Since he first started going to Spurs, the club as an organisation has changed beyond recognition. 'Spurs is the English football club model,' he says. 'It was the family firm, the local firm of undistinguished businessmen as I understood it; funeral directors or butchers or something, some of them, but Spurs became the archetype, the first quoted, the first live game on telly . . . I think Spurs have definitely changed, no different from anybody else. It's more business-orientated.'

The mixed feelings Bruce harbours about this new, more corporate, side to the game are not uncommon.

'I always thought it was slightly distasteful, all this business of adverts on the telly and pictures of Spurs stars in the Stock Exchange and stuff,' he says. 'I thought it was all a bit naff, but there was also a certain amount of pride in it. I think we tried to be a forward-thinking club, but then you started spotting them investing in bra-making companies.' When this period of history is discussed, one name is unavoidable – that of former chairman Irving Scholar. 'Apparently he's written in his book that it's all everyone else's fault, which I suspect is the idea of autobiographies,' laughs Bruce, who traces the change in his relationship with the club he'd followed since he was so young to Scholar's most controversial idea – replacing the popular Shelf terrace with executive boxes.

'Some of the ideas he had were good, but it was the "Left on the Shelf" campaign that was the first time I ever remember being overtly critical of the club. I wasn't really as passionate as anybody else, but I remember going to a couple of meetings at Wood Green Civic Centre. So that would have been the start of it and from then it just went on, right up to the Sugar years. We were on a high, really, all the build-up to the FA Cup final in '91, and there was the question of the club maybe not even existing and people getting really jumpy. I had a mate who was a Midland Bank manager telling me, "It's not looking good", and he could see the accounts.

'We're only just starting to get out of all that, really. Maybe still being a quoted company is a double-edged sword because a lot of the washing is done in public – which is ultimately for the good. I'm getting some encouraging signs now. I'd like to think we've had our share of fans with no business idea and businessmen with no idea of being a fan to perhaps a happy medium – but then I am one of life's optimists.'

It's also often been said that Spurs fans harp on about the past so much it becomes a burden. Bruce reckons that's an easier point to respond to. 'I'm one of the traditionalists,' he admits. 'I think we should celebrate what we had: it's why we go. I'm so old now, I saw some of it, so that's probably why I keep going back, it keeps me grounded. Otherwise, why wouldn't any football fan switch to Man U or Arsenal? I think some of our fans have lost touch with reality a bit, in terms of continually saying, "We're a big club," because you're going to get the response: "Well, bloody prove it." But if that puts pressure on people to keep performing to a certain standard, then I don't think it can be a negative influence because I don't think you should accept that we're going to be also-rans.'

This seems as good a time as any to return solely to football matters and the question of who Bruce's favourites on the pitch have been.

'I suppose it would have to be Glenn Hoddle. Across my era he just was so special; he was a very, very good player who was there for a long time. Then Ardiles, Mabbutt for different reasons, Ricky Villa was a particular favourite of mine, Steve Archibald, Chris Waddle . . . I got into hero worship long after I should have done, because there were a couple of seasons when Chris Waddle could do things with a football that you'd thought you'd forgotten.'

For favourite games, Bruce chooses two very different ones. The first would be near the top of any Spurs fan's list; the second many would rather forget. Nevertheless, his choices neatly illustrate the range of pleasures fans draw from following their club.

'One-off games I think would probably be the semi-final against Arsenal in '91. Coming home from that game with my mate in the car (we were going to do our celebrating later) and just seeing normal grounded people waiting for buses and people walking the streets, I said, "Look at them, they can't know, they obviously don't know what's just gone on round the corner there." It was just like sheer nirvana.'

Bruce's second choice is the unsuccessful trip to Kaiserslautern in Tottenham's all-too-brief return to Europe in 1999, a trip which he undertook with a large group of fans, including one of the writers of this book. We flew out early on the morning of the game and met up with various friends who've become regular travelling companions over the last 15 years or so. It was a peaceful, friendly trip, and we'll remember the kindness and hospitality of the local people – who'd apparently been rather apprehensive about our arrival – for some time. Thanks to this, the efforts of a fluent German-speaker in our party, and some fantastic food and beer, we'd had a great day out – so more's the pity a typically negative George Graham side paid the price by conceding a last-minute own-goal to go out of the competition.

'The trip to Kaiserslautern in '99 I immensely enjoyed,' says Bruce, 'especially when you contrast that from a football perspective. That's one of the darker moments. People were crying on the terrace, and I could feel it, you know. I wasn't far off it myself. To concede an own-goal, to go out when you were singing about who you were going to get in the next round, it's all what football's about. You know, a football experience is a kick in the ribs as much as a leap into the roof, but I still look back on that trip as absolutely fantastic.'

So, what does Bruce expect to see happen to his club in the next few years, and is this far from what he wants? There's a familiar struggle between fantasy and reality played out in his answer. 'What I'd like to see happen is we get wedged in behind as a third or fourth or fifth most successful club in the English League. Well, no, obviously if I'm honest, what I'd want is to win the League in my lifetime. But if I'm being realistic with what I want, I would say I want us to get into Europe on a regular basis, carry on on the trophy trail in terms of cup competitions, and to stay in touching distance of the big three.'

As the new season dawned, Bruce was about to be reminded how difficult even that limited ambition would be to achieve.

2

The King of White Hart Lane:
Lee Benjamin

Hoddle, Hoddle
Hoddle, Hoddle
Born is the King of White Hart Lane

Tottenham Hotspur fans have become used to viewing each season as transitional. Ours is a team that always seems to be on the way to somewhere, but never arrives. In August 2003, there was at least a sense that things would be different.

It was the beginning of manager Glenn Hoddle's third full season in charge and make or break time not just for a former playing hero but also for the club itself. Failure to qualify for Europe or improve on the familiar midtable finish would confirm that Spurs had slipped down the pecking order behind the likes of Bolton, Blackburn and Southampton. It would also probably mean the end of Hoddle's tenure at the club. Hoddle's appointment had been seen by many fans, and choreographed by the board, as the prodigal's return: one of the club's greatest-ever players and a proven coach taking the tiller and steering Spurs back to the big time with a flourish. If he failed, where would the club turn?

These dark thoughts of failure can't have been far from any Spurs fan's mind as the season began. The side had finished the previous campaign with a series of dreadful performances and some bizarre comments from Hoddle – most notably his insistence that Spurs had 'dominated' an away game against Middlesbrough that they lost 5–1, apparently due to four lucky goals. A comprehensive beating at the hands of Blackburn Rovers in the final home game of the season led to angry fans showering the pitch with used season-ticket books, and Hoddle had only just survived an inquest into his position at a board meeting.

The summer provided better news. Having decided to back their manager, the board gave him the money to buy the players he wanted. So in came highly rated Portuguese striker Helder Postiga; Bobby Zamora, generally considered the best forward outside the Premiership; and former West Ham hitman Freddie Kanouté. In addition, a number of high-earning but ageing players were offloaded.

All this was cause for optimism, but the more a manager gets what he wants the less excuse there is for failure. Few fans thought Hoddle was perfect: his man-management skills did appear to leave something to be desired, and he seemed at times to demonstrate a stubborn refusal to recognise problems that stared him in the face. Until now, however, he had been working with a set of players he'd inherited rather than one he'd created; he'd been hampered by the club's infamous injury problems; and he'd generally not had the time to establish his regime. But this was Hoddle's squad now, playing Hoddle's tactics over enough time to expect some sign of progress to manifest itself.

This combination of factors, together with the loathing large sections of the press harboured towards Hoddle, meant he was the bookies' favourite to be the first manager to lose his job in the new season. It should be pointed out that the rumour that a corps of leading football journalists dislikes Hoddle has substance. Stemming from his time as England manager, Hoddle has never been forgiven for deceiving the press over injury news and team selection – a cardinal sin as far as the sports desks are concerned. One tabloid journalist went so far as to tell the authors of this book: 'They really hate Hoddle. When he left the England job, they were slapping each other on the back congratulating themselves.'

It is true that sections of the press were anticipating Hoddle's failure with glee, but neither manager nor club had done themselves any favours through the clumsy manner in which they dealt with the press. Hoddle barely concealed his disdain for them, thus accentuating the image of an aloof figure who viewed those around him as somehow lacking. Furthermore, the club had acquired a reputation for attempting to lay false trails which had served only to ensure everything it said was treated with cynicism.

Contrary to the stories appearing in the press, the club's fans were still overwhelmingly behind Hoddle. A few had wobbled at the end of the previous season, but now he was leading a squad which included £34 million-worth of his own buys – with £12 million spent that summer – into a new campaign. It was the moment of truth.

Spurs opened with a 1–0 defeat at Birmingham that highlighted one of the fans' major worries – they did not have a midfield ball-winner. But this was a new team, and the following week it began to gel, beating Leeds at home 2–1 with a fine fightback from a goal down. An excellent performance at Anfield saw Liverpool held 0–0, which only left a very winnable game against Fulham at home to send Spurs into the week's break for internationals with a comfortable 7 points from 12. Instead, Spurs utterly collapsed to a Fulham side widely tipped for relegation, losing 3–0 in a performance reminiscent of the shambles at the end of the previous season. Afterwards, Hoddle complained that international call-ups meant he wouldn't be able to work things out with his defence on the training ground, despite the fact that he'd had two years to work things out and that only one of his defenders was on international duty.

'No one likes to see a manager hounded out of his job,' wrote Paul MacInnes in *The Guardian* after the Fulham game. An enduring football cliché is that when a boss receives the board's vote of confidence, it's time for him to start checking the Situations Vacant column. Perhaps a better indicator of the impending sack is when the hacks start feeling sorry for the victim.

Unfortunately for Hoddle, the season resumed against Chelsea at Stamford Bridge, a side Spurs hadn't beaten in the League for 27 games, and one which was now stuffed with world-class talent, thanks to billionaire Roman Abramovich. A Spurs victory would have been a major surprise, so there was plenty of time to pen the 'Hoddle in crisis' pieces that would inevitably follow. Sure enough, Spurs lost 4–2 and the 'Hoddle to go' stories poured forth. Hoddle's response to a post-match question about lack of leadership on the pitch – 'Leadership starts from within' – illuminated no one and prompted Paul MacInnes to observe that, once again, the manager was 'making things difficult for himself'. But Hoddle didn't need to. His side's next game was at home to Southampton, the club he'd left in rancorous circumstances to take over at Spurs. The Saints were unbeaten, and Spurs needed maximum points.

Instead, they lost three points in a humiliating game, and that weekend it took one brief phone call (reportedly lasting just 30 seconds) from honeymooning chairman Daniel Levy and Glenn Hoddle – Saint Glenn, the King of White Hart Lane – was sacked.

It was a sad end to a sad saga. Few among the Tottenham fans expressed any glee at such a fall from grace. If there was a consensus, something always notoriously difficult to gauge, it was that Hoddle had to go – but his departure was not a cause for celebration. The question most were asking was how had it come to such a pass. Indeed, for many, Hoddle was the Messiah. Two and a half years later, he was at least halfway there. Spurs were a mess.

For all the goodwill that fans invested in Hoddle, the harsh, unavoidable truth is that he failed. Having spent £34 million in two and half years, and backed by a loyal support that never once publicly turned on their hero, Hoddle had created a side almost indistinguishable from its predecessors over the last ten years: inconsistent, underachieving and far too often an easy touch for other teams.

When the boos rang out on the final whistle at home to Southampton, they were not for the manager but for the downcast players. However, the inference was clear – Hoddle's team were simply not up to scratch. Despite a brief rally inspired by Robbie Keane and topped with another Kanouté goal, Southampton's earlier third had sealed the result and, with it, Hoddle's fate. According to touch-line witnesses, he turned to his faithful assistant John Gorman and said, 'I'm out of a job.' He was proved correct when, 24 hours later, Levy's 'Dear John' phone call ended the affair.

The aftermath proved surprising. Certainly, journalists with a longstanding antipathy to 'Glenda' warmed their hands once again over the ashes of another demise, Alan Green giving an obvious game away on Radio 5's *606* with the gleefully delivered comment that, 'there won't be too many in the media sad to see Hoddle go'.

But by and large, the press reaction was sympathetic, illustrated best by Steven Howard's column in *The Sun*, in which he offered his condolences to Hoddle, choosing instead to criticise the fans and directors. This wasn't the usual Spurs-bashing that incenses Tottenham fans but an expression of an uncomfortable truth: most Spurs fans had wanted Hoddle; now they were reaping what they had sown.

The more immediate issue of Hoddle's sacking, however, was the timing. Many questioned why, after being given £12 million to spend in the summer, he had been given just six games to turn things around. Nearly a month after he left, Hoddle himself broke his silence, to muse on just the same question.

However, Hoddle wasn't sacked because of six games; he had been ditched for eighteen months of failure in which the team made no progress. The decline of Hoddle's Spurs can be traced back to the Worthington Cup final defeat of 2002, but the final record of three wins in his last sixteen games told its own story. Perhaps the board should have dispensed with Hoddle in the summer of 2003 when he just survived a seven-hour inquest; maybe the final judgement is that they did at least act before matters deteriorated even further.

For a brief period, Spurs were once again leading the sports news – even if it was in circumstances no fan had particularly wanted. With David Pleat stepping into the breach once more as caretaker manager, Spurs supporters headed off to see their team survive a potentially tricky Carling Cup tie with a comfortable 3–0 win at Coventry. This was followed by a lucky goalless draw at Manchester City, before a thumping 3–0 home win over Everton, the latter featuring a potential goal-of-the-season from Kanouté.

There were two conclusions to be drawn from this mini-revival. The first was that the fans continued to sing Hoddle's name, and so his standing as a Spurs legend had clearly survived his failings as a manager. The second was that, crucially, in those three games, Spurs kept a trio of clean sheets, engineered in the main by Pleat's decision to revert to an orthodox 4–4–2.

Pleat, so often cited as one of the problems in the club's power structure for his allegedly 'difficult' relationship with Hoddle, charmed the media with a succession of rueful smiles and enigmatic comments as to his own future, but he had made his point.

As for Hoddle? Any sympathy he may have gained from fans and neutrals for his initially dignified reaction to his sacking were undone somewhat by later comments. Try as he might not to sound bitter, Hoddle sounded just that, particularly with the ludicrous claim that he had been planning to adopt Pleat's preferred formation all along, coupled with the familiar 'not me, guv' attitude in distancing himself from his squad's failures.

It was par for the course. Throughout his spell as manager,

Hoddle had clutched at excuses while claiming they weren't, in fact, excuses. Complaining about a freakish injury list was justifiable; constant moans about poor refereeing decisions, poor tactics, naming and blaming individual players, and laughable claims of bad luck, such as the 5–1 defeat at Boro, were anything but justifiable.

Perhaps Hoddle's fundamental flaw was that, in his genuine love for Spurs, he felt passion and love alone were enough. Time and again, and indeed since his sacking, Hoddle made a point of proclaiming his credentials as a Tottenham fan. Few fans, however, have a minute's silence before a home game for their dad, as Hoddle did when his father died in 2002. The contrast with the unforgivable mistake in not having a similar tribute the following season for Len Duquemin, veteran of the 1951 Championship-winning team, who died in April 2003, spoke volumes.

It wasn't Hoddle's fault that Tottenham's infamous PR department had 'made the decision' not to remember a club great, but maybe Hoddle *was* to blame in giving the impression one man actually *did* think he was bigger than the club.

Lee Benjamin is a Tottenham fan of over 40 years' standing who's seen it all – but even he was taken aback by the rapid demise of his all-time favourite, Glenn Hoddle.

'Glenn the player remains a Spurs legend and always will, but the last few years have seriously tarnished his name. As a player, he was first class, and he arrived to the acclaim of most Spurs fans, but I doubt that anyone would have seen him making such a balls-up of the job in such a short time,' says Lee.

'The sacking was inevitable – it should have been done in May 2003 when it was obvious that he'd lost the plot. A lot of people accused ex-players of sour grapes when they talked about his man-management and communication skills – but that's utter crap.'

A typically forthright opinion from a supporter never likely to stand on ceremony – one who, according to the stereotype, is the archetypal Spurs fan. Aged 50, Jewish, raised in Stamford Hill just up the road from White Hart Lane and now living on the east London–Essex border, this is a fan who wears his Spurs identity like a glove. To cap it all, he's a qualified taxi driver.

Legend has it that every cabbie in London is a Tottenham fan. It's a myth, of course, but received wisdom dictates that, from Romford to Ilford, the capital's legion of licensed cabbies pour out on to the streets of the city every day to hold forth on politics, sport and life in general, and all of them with Tottenham mini-kits swinging from their rear-view mirror.

In some respects, Lee Benjamin lives up to the billing. He's opinionated, conservative with a big and small 'c', doesn't suffer fools gladly and could talk for England given half the chance. He's a musician, a regular contributor to local radio and has set up his own website, 'Spurs Views'. But whatever the subject, when it comes to voicing opinions, Lee Benjamin is never backward in coming forward.

He continues his assessment of the Hoddle situation: 'The legacy of Hoddle's reign, well, it's not impressive. Hod had tried to form a midfield in the same image as the one he played in, but he managed one with a lack of ability to retain the ball, or to pass it accurately. Then there's the sub-standard players that constituted his defence. Couple that lot to formations that were suicidal and a set of tactics that the players simply didn't understand, and, *voilà*, you got the entirely expected result – a team in the relegation zone.

'It's right that he was sacked before the damage became irreversible, but what were we left with after two and a half years and over £30 million spent? Sadly, we were worse off than when [George] Graham was in charge, as our squad had reduced in quality.'

It was enough to set Lee off on a typically strident but well-argued tangent about the wider state of play at Spurs.

'Like it or loathe it, we are in the situation we are now, and we've got to work within that. I do believe we should be running things on a business footing, because if we go under we've got nothing left. Can you imagine no Spurs? It's unthinkable. So we have to stay in business. But, in my opinion, we have gone right down to the tight-fisted-arsehole end of the scale. We're not even trying. The club has been in gradual decline for 20 years and events have seen hardly anything to turn that decline around.'

For Lee, the 2003–04 season did present the unthinkable. After decades as a season-ticket holder, he finally decided enough was enough. When the renewal forms were sent out by the club, Lee's ended up in the bin.

'Every single person on this planet has a breaking point. I reached mine in May 2003. Forty-four years ago, I started watching Blanchflower, Mackay, Jones and White. The season before last concluded with a midfield of something like Gus, Bunjy, Shaggy and Toda. Well, not on my fucking money!

'I've got no doubt that it won't be long before I return as a season-ticket holder, but before that happens, I would need to be convinced that the board *really* mean to take Spurs forward.'

It's a familiar refrain from Spurs fans jaded by endless seasons of transition and underachievement. But the strength of Lee's opinions also stem from an intimate knowledge of his club, formed over five decades of unwavering support. Like many of his contemporaries, he had a good introduction.

'I started going in August 1960, which was the start of the season we won the Double,' he says. 'I got dragged along to a game by an older cousin who was a Spurs supporter. My mum and dad, they had no interest in it all. I'd never been before in my life, came down here, found I liked it and grew to love it. When I walked into White Hart Lane for the first time, I didn't know dick about football. I just learned about the game from when I watched it for the first time. I thought I'd go along and give it a try, and, well, the rest is history.'

In the first few years of Lee's support of Spurs, that history ranks as the most productive and glorious period in Tottenham's 120-year existence. Spurs didn't just win the hitherto 'impossible' Double of League and Cup, they set records along the way and used the all-conquering season as the launch pad for further success, notably by becoming the first British side to lift a European trophy. Above all, though, they won the Double in the defining style of 'the Spurs Way'.

'The reputation of Spurs was world class at the time,' says Lee. 'Arguably, the best in the world. Spurs had done something that hadn't been done for many years, scoring over 100 goals, which was also a rarity. They just had quality players throughout the team, from back to front.'

Latterday supporters used to the more prosaic talents seen in recent years might as well have been watching a different sport to the Double generation. But if the quality of football was different, the experience of being a fan was another ball game altogether. From muddy pitch to PLC boardroom, Lee has witnessed the transformation in the fortunes of Spurs in particular and the game in general.

'Football is very much in your face now – TV, radio and that,' he said. 'If there's a big football story, it's front-page news, whereas in those days, it never got off the back pages. Football was very low profile when I started going.'

It's another football cliché that the atmosphere was better in the old days – massed ranks of men in flat caps with never a hint of crowd trouble to worry them, screaming in the high-pitched roar that seems an indelible feature of the old newsreels. However, it's an idealised image that Lee is happy to confirm.

'Aah, the atmosphere was absolutely incredible: it was just like a wall of noise. I used to get to the ground at 11.30 a.m., otherwise I wouldn't get my little perch in the front of the Shelf, right up against the fence, 'cos I was only a little lad then. But the atmosphere was amazing. I can remember that the noise then would blow you away. I honestly think it frightened a lot of opposition teams.

'There was no "organised" chanting as far as I can remember. The club certainly weren't printing song lyrics in the programme, blaring it out in all the speakers before the game as they do now. It was just general shouting and screaming your head off and giving the ref some stick, that sort of thing. It was very intense.'

To follow Spurs today, the paying spectator needs to part with up to £55 for a single game. For the young Benjamin it was a more modest one and sixpence, 'or seven and a half pence as it would be today, to get in and stand on the Shelf, and I think a programme was about tuppence'. But Lee has no nostalgic illusions about the creature comforts of the old White Hart Lane, aware that today's all-seater stadia offer improved facilities.

'You knew it was a big ground, but if you actually looked at the seating areas in the Paxton and Park Lane, it looked like they'd been put together with bits of plywood. The other thing I remember is that when you went to reserve games and sat in the old West Stand, you thought you felt uncomfortable because you weren't used to sitting in such luxury, but even back then the ground looked a bit ramshackle, not in the greatest of nick. But it didn't really matter – you were worried about team matters, the players.'

Another sign of how dramatically things have changed since the early 1960s heyday is that Lee recalls Tottenham's rivals as sides like Burnley, Blackpool, Sheffield Wednesday and even Leyton Orient – 'they were pretty much like the modern-day Bolton'. Liverpool were just beginning their Shankly-inspired rise to the top, while Manchester United were a familiar big-name presence. But tellingly, in a clear reversal of the current situation, Arsenal played a notable second fiddle to their north London neighbours.

It's enough to warm a Spurs fan's heart. In the 1960s, the Gunners were overshadowed by a rampant Tottenham team that ranked as the best in the country – though such pre-eminence proved short-lived.

'During the '60s, we were *the* club; during the '70s, it was fairly even, which was a good thing: we could go to Highbury with half a chance of getting a result. As long as you had a bit of genuine hope, you were happy. Of course, when we go to Highbury these days – it ain't exactly a cheerful prospect, is it?'

It's a theme Lee returns to again and again – how good it used to be to follow Spurs, and by default how underwhelming it has so often been through the 1990s and now into the twenty-first century. Those fans reared on the frequently depressed mood of more recent crowds can only wonder at the sheer thrill of happier times.

'It was a great place to be then. It was friendly, it was fun, it was very upbeat. Obviously, the team's results pretty much influenced the mood of the crowd. And we were doing well, right the way up to the '80s, when we was nicking a cup now and again. We played a decent style of football, we was always able to sign decent players. Things were always positive.'

So what of the criticism that Spurs fans dwell too much on the past? 'Bollocks. The fans talk about the history and that's right. You've got to know what you're talking about. When anybody first starts supporting the club, then anything from that moment on becomes part of your history and the club's history. And you can't talk about that too much, that's what football fans do. That's in the blood, that's part of the game.'

Nonetheless, it's clear that the consistent failures of the last decade have marked a decisive shift in how Lee perceives his right as a fan to complain.

'Maybe we're a bit more vociferous than most, but I don't remember us being as critical then [pre-1990s] as we were in the latter stages of Uncle Al's reign. Of course, when you lose a game, you moan, go home, kick the dog; but years ago we weren't looking at the same mediocre players like we have been of late. In those days, we'd go out and buy a Martin Chivers or a Paul Gascoigne or a Gary Lineker – we would go and buy players of that quality if the team started flagging. We don't go and get players now. We're not addressing that problem – and it's down to evil lucre.'

The old problem of money. Of all the issues that have rattled and riled fans since the game began its renaissance in the early 1990s, probably none has caused so much anger, resentment and debate as the question of finance and in particular the rapid increase in players' wages. As their remuneration has increased, funded as ever through the wallets and purses of supporters, so expectations have also risen – though Lee is at pains to point out that he does not deny a player's right to big money.

'If you go back to the days when I first started going to football, the balance of wealth was with the club. The players were very much second-class citizens; the minimum wage had barely gone.

'Put it into perspective. Jimmy Greaves signed for Spurs for 60 nicker a week; he was actually offered 120 nicker a week by West Ham, but he turned it down because he wanted to come and play for Spurs. Now we find out from Daniel Levy that the Thomson [shirt sponsorship] money covered Jamie Redknapp's wages. So we're talking about Jamie earning about a million and a quarter a year – the balance has shifted from players earning a comparatively small amount to them now earning an absolute fortune.

'There needed to be a power shift because players were getting paid bugger all, and I don't know about most fans, but I'll be paying money to watch the players, not some accountant going through the latest balance sheet. So it's right that the people we get to entertain us are the ones who are earning a decent and fair wage.

'Listen, if someone turned round to me and said, "Drive a cab around for 50 grand a week", I wouldn't say no. I certainly don't blame them for taking what they're offered. All I can ask, though, is when the bloke puts on his shirt for my club, he goes out and he gives it everything he can.'

Embittered by the saga that led to former captain Sol Campbell moving to rivals Arsenal on a free transfer ('Why couldn't he have just been honest?'), Lee's attitude towards players has fundamentally altered. Where once he treated footballers like Dave Mackay, Cliff Jones and his all-time favourite Glenn Hoddle as his heroes, they have now become distant, well-paid but temporary employees, neither loved nor believed.

We Are Tottenham

If the relationship between player and fans has fundamentally altered, then so too has the association between supporters and directors. The role of those who own and run the club, at least at Tottenham, has been transformed. Today, chairmen, directors and chief executives are omnipresent participants in the media circus.

'Criticism and praise went straight to the managers and the players,' says Lee of the old days. 'The board were completely out of the equation. They did put their money in, but back then you didn't know they were there.'

For Lee, directors were inconspicuous trustees of the club who obligingly wrote cheques to sign the likes of Jimmy Greaves. 'When you looked at the players brought through in those years, it was obvious that the business was solvent and well run and that we had the funds to buy people. They done a great job. You could name at most half a dozen chairmen back then. Nowadays they're celebrities, aren't they?'

Times have clearly changed. Arguably, it is Tottenham that did the most to promote such a root-and-branch shift in the way the game is run. Long before Manchester United became a worldwide brand with a football team to operate as a marketing tool, Spurs were in the vanguard of the financial revolution, the first club to become a PLC. It's not on Lee's list of glorious Tottenham achievements.

'It was Irving Scholar started this off,' Lee recalls with a resigned sigh. 'The man's motives were absolutely pure – he loved the club, would have done anything for us. But as a businessman – total prat. Him, in 1983, making us the pioneers on the stock market, was the worst day's work ever done for football, never mind us, because it puts the club at the mercy of anyone who comes along with enough money – and lo and behold, along came Sir Alan [Sugar]. Which to me was like ten years of purgatory.

'I mean, staff-wise and player-wise he took over a reasonably good football club. Financially we were in a mess, but operationally we were in pretty good nick. And he actually allowed that to decline to a state where we're a midtable team now. With huge potential, it has to be said, but that for me is the real kick – you know, we've lost the drive and the ambition to be up there with the real big clubs. Not the fans, I hasten to add, I mean the club, under the board, have lost that ambition. It's all about staying up and getting the money off of Sky. That ain't bloody good enough.'

When Sugar was finally deposed as owner of Tottenham, with investment company Enic taking his place, hope once again sprang eternal for Spurs supporters. In Daniel Levy as chairman, they saw someone who understood the traditions, expectations and demands of the club taking the helm.

Almost four years later, Levy and Enic have steered Spurs through the all too familiar course of midtable underachievement. Lee was willing to give them a chance but remains sceptical. Perhaps too many seasons of disappointment have lowered expectations?

'I expect the club to do what they said they were going to do. They've said they've got this five-year plan, they're going to take it easy, they're not going to get in debt, they're going to run the business on the side of caution. Fine, you need to do that, but you must be putting players on the park while you're doing so, and you've got to be getting a little bit better every season.'

Like their predecessors, the issue with Levy's regime is not that it hasn't spent money. Far from it: Tottenham have supplied a succession of managers with around £100 million of investment in the last decade. The problem is that the money has been badly spent.

'We've had so many mediocre players, it's unbelievable. You can start off with Jason Dozzell. We got mugged for a fortune for him. I remember when it was announced we'd signed him, along with thousands of others, I was saying, "Who the fuck's Jason Dozzell?" Never heard of the guy, but we paid £1.7 million for him and when he turned up we now know why we never heard of him – he was crap.

'But take the squad we've had for the last few years. We signed players like Tim Sherwood for God's sake. It's farcical, it's absolutely farcical and allegedly he was earning £18,000 a week, which for a player who contributed as little as he did is absolutely ludicrous. But it's the going rate.'

While directors grapple with balance sheets and share prices, transfer fees and a punishing wage bill, any discussion about money and football invariably comes back to the role television now plays. With the advent of Sky and the massive television deals that followed, the British game has been transformed, arguably to the cost of the club that pioneered its commercialisation. But if some fans regard Sky as the root of football's excesses, Lee is not about to join them.

'I think Sky has been absolutely excellent for the game: the presentation and the coverage is second to none. You would never ever have seen it with the likes of the Beeb and ITV in a million years if Sky hadn't actually come into the market and challenged their privileged and totally underused position.

'So I take my hat off to them. Listen, I don't like going to football at 2 p.m. on a Sunday afternoon any more than the next man. But if you're paying the sort of money out that they are, I absolutely respect their right to say, "We've got a slot where we'd like to put a game into."'

One recent choice that Lee Benjamin has made – other than to ditch his season ticket – is to break his usual habits and become increasingly supportive of fans' groups. Armed with a radical agenda in response to the way they perceive the game is being taken away from them, and using the medium provided by the fanzines that emerged in the late 1980s, supporters – small in number, but well organised – have become increasingly proactive in trying to influence how their clubs are run.

Tottenham fans have been at the forefront of this phenomenon. Sparked in the main by the unpopular redevelopment of the beloved Shelf terrace in the late 1980s and then by the divisive court battle between Alan Sugar and Terry Venables in 1993, supporters formed pressure groups such as Left on the Shelf, the Tottenham Action Group and the Tottenham Independent Supporters' Association, the latter the first of its kind and the role model for subsequent supporter groups. Latterly, the various bodies have coalesced into the Tottenham Hotspur Supporters' Trust (THST), an early example of the kind and one of the biggest supporters' trusts in the country.

There is still an awful long way to go before it can be said that fans are able to call the shots. Nevertheless, in true foot-in-the-door fashion, the average fan does now at least have a chance to make his or her voice heard. At Spurs, the Trust has been officially recognised by the club and formal communication channels have been established in the shape of meetings with directors and management and open 'Q&A' evenings.

Proof that things have changed can be seen in the fact that fans like Lee have got involved. Where once he was almost scathing of the agenda and effectiveness of supporter bodies, he now believes they can make a difference.

'With the organisations that have gone before, they've all had a very negative slant about them, you know, get Sugar out, etc. – good luck to them, these are sentiments I share, but nevertheless it was all on the destructive side of the balance sheet, whereas the current Trust is very much on the positive mode.

'They're set up for the right reasons: they want us to be able to communicate with the club and tell them our moans, and where possible we may see that some of the things we've moaned about will get put right. The club are prepared to listen to us because we're not just here to be kicked in the teeth; we're here to talk to them about real issues.'

Lee didn't just join the THST; he has become an active member, culminating in his stint as membership secretary. With an inside view of the organisation, he talks with the zeal of a committed believer.

'There are many members (or prospective members) who would tell you that things are not going well for the Trust. I believe that if you confront the boss of a company with the comment that he/she doesn't have the foggiest how to run their business, you're liable to be met with hostility. Despite contrary opinions, THST has excellent channels of communication with the club and we are being listened to. It's not always necessary to carry a big stick.'

As a veteran, Lee has witnessed some truly awful times, but perhaps surprisingly, the relegation season of 1976–77 does not represent his Tottenham nadir. 'A lot of people will frown upon this but not me: pretty nearly every game we played under George Graham, watching the way the team were going, was absolute hell – to see my beloved Tottenham Hotspur play football like that. The whole Spurs ethos was just kicked in the arse and thrown out the window.

'There's no particular game – well, actually, I dunno, the 0–0 at home to Man City. Games like that they could have played for 900 minutes and neither team would have scored. Playing in that manner, honestly, I can't think of another period as bad as that. Even the team that went down came straight back up again playing good football.'

It is, of course, the good times that make such long periods of misery all worthwhile, but Lee's nomination for his greatest

Tottenham experience is a surprise. 'Well, going through every single emotion, you'd have to say the European Cup semi-final when we played Benfica here and just missed out on getting to the final – all because of one poxy goal.

'We went through everything in that game. There was joy, there was despair, there was elation. And, of course, back then Benfica were, like Spurs, a truly great side. A real battle of the giants, and that was just the most incredible game.

'The other one for me was an FA Cup replay in 1967 when we won the Cup, against Millwall of all people. There were 70,000 people in here. When we did score the winner, no one could throw their hands up in the air because we were so packed in. That one sticks in the mind because we'd drawn at their place, weren't particularly great, then beat them here and we felt we could go on and win the Cup, which we did – against Chelsea, which was quite pleasing!'

A typical Spurs fan's response – never happier than when his or her team lose one game heroically and win in slightly unconventional circumstances. If there is a defining characteristic that makes a Tottenham supporter, then perhaps it is this: a masochistic willingness to revel in glory and despair, usually at the same time. Lee would deny such a trait, but there's an incident that happened during of one of the hundreds of matches he's seen that perhaps sums up the attitudes of White Hart Lane's long-suffering, long-complaining patrons.

'My first season ticket at Spurs was the '78–'79 season, just after we got the Argentinians out of the World Cup. Now that was in the Upper East, we were home to Southampton, it was winter, and it was a God-awful day.

'We were fairly central, more or less right behind the TV gantry, and right over in block A, which was on the corner with Park Lane, my brother-in-law had his seat there and his mate Big Barry. So we said we'd meet them over there at half-time. As we were strolling towards Barry's seat, there was what seemed like a big, big scuffle down by the front, and as we got a bit closer there was several people holding a guy by his ankles and he was suspended head-first facing the terrace of the Shelf below.

'And the man, apparently, I'd gathered from the screams I'd heard, had definitely intended to fall over and commit suicide. He had the shits, the guy wanted to end it all, right there and then, in the East Stand at White Hart Lane. Eventually, he was dragged back, but he's going, "Let me go, I want to die, I wanna go," and all this sort of thing. Anyway, the Old Bill arrived and he calmed down a bit before someone shouted out, "The game ain't that fucking bad, is it?'"

3

We're gonna be in that number:
Mally Armstrong and Tommy Edmondson

Oh when the Spurs
Go marching in
Oh when the Spurs
Go marching in
We're gonna be in that number
When the Spurs go marching in

After what seemed to have been an extraordinarily long break for internationals, in mid-October the rhythm of the domestic programme was finally set to establish itself. So far, Spurs fans had seen a start, a stop, a restart, a sacking and a stop. As the evenings were beginning to draw in, it was heads down for the long haul.

An indication of just how long it would be came as Spurs resumed their season away at Leicester. The fact that it was live on Sky was not a good omen: in recent years Spurs have reserved some of their most inept performances for live broadcasts.

Sure enough, at 70 minutes, Leicester, bottom of the table and already looking destined for relegation, led 1–0 and Spurs looked a shambles. Then David Pleat changed things around with some substitutions, something Spurs fans hadn't seen for some time. On came Mbulelo Mabizela and Bobby Zamora, both summer signings, and within minutes the pair had combined to put Spurs level, Zamora's perfect pass enabling Mabizela to belt a 25-yarder into the net. It was the South African's first goal for the club, and his ecstatic, shirt-kissing reaction in front of the travelling support suggested there was at least some feeling for the club on a playing staff that too often looked uninterested. In the final minute, top scorer Freddie Kanouté grabbed a winner to seal an unlikely victory and preserve Pleat's unbeaten record. The closing stages of the match also saw Kanouté carried off after a reckless challenge from City's Muzzy Izzet, and it was this challenge, rather than the team's explosive fightback, that was to prove most influential in the coming weeks.

Although Pleat's unbeaten run had been preserved courtesy of changes rung by him, it hadn't gone unnoticed that the subs who turned the game were signed by Hoddle. The point, raised at the post-match press conference, seemed to annoy Pleat, who remarked that, 'a month ago we would have lost that [game]'.

Until that moment, Pleat had been a canny operator with the press, perhaps out of necessity. He couldn't say he wanted the manager's job permanently in case the board went for someone else, as his declared ambition would make any new manager identify him as a threat. Yet, if he really did want the job, he couldn't underplay his hand either. But Pleat wouldn't have been human if he didn't react testily to the suggestion that his success in turning the team around was really down to the man he replaced, and soon he and Hoddle were embroiled in a war of words. Pleat told journalists that the board had a number of criteria upon which it was basing its search, including, 'Is he a nutter?' He went on to say that the players hadn't understood Hoddle's 3–5–2 formation and criticised Hoddle for wanting to show he was still the best in training rather than standing back and observing his charges.

As the story blew up, Pleat offered the standard defence of being 'quoted out of context', but inside sources reported the board as being livid that he'd been drawn into this. Hoddle wasn't slow to hit back, saying Pleat 'was so obstructive towards me, never working in harmony with me and always working towards his own end. Let him take on the responsibility and, without his disruptive intervention behind the scenes, the fans might just get their success.'

The smoke from this latest Tottenham personality duel had hardly had time to clear before fresh events rocked the club. Finance director Paul Viner abruptly left amid rumours that Spurs were about to post heavy losses. It soon emerged that the board was split over Daniel Levy's plan to raise more money for the club. As faction briefed against faction, it seemed affairs were returning to what passes for normal at the club.

On the pitch, the unbeaten run continued, but only just, as Spurs hosted Middlesbrough – again live on TV – in what was quickly dubbed the most boring match in the history of the Premier League. Not only was the fare served up exceptionally poor, Spurs were lucky to come out of it with a point.

Two fans in the crowd that day had particular reason to be disappointed. Mally Armstrong, 43, and Tommy Edmondson, 50, live in Carlisle, about as far from Tottenham as it's possible to get in England. For them, there are no home games.

'It was a bit of a lie-in for us today,' says Mally. 'Seven o'clock start because we're coming down in the car, so you're up at six o'clock getting organised. Traffic was good today, got down here half past twelve, so that's five and a half hours. It's midnight when you're getting home, and then if it's a Saturday game, I work nearly every Sunday, so it's a case of getting home at midnight, going to bed, getting up at five o' clock then working six till two on a Sunday.'

It's not just a case of getting themselves to Tottenham either. The two men run the Northern Spurs Supporters' Club: Mally is the chairman and Tommy is the treasurer.

'Today there's nine of us come down,' explains Mally. 'There's two from Carlisle, two from Kendal, one from Chorley, one from Preston, one from Wigan and another two lads from Prestwich.

'I think last season I covered 25 games home and away. It's ongoing 'cos you're booking tickets six weeks in advance, you're always in contact on the phone or you get newsletters and send newsletters out and try and keep everybody in touch. We're officially recognised by the club. This season we've got about 72 members. There's some from the Scots side, Dumfries, and as far down as, well, Wigan's about the farthest south that we have members.

'You've got to be a member of Spurs before you can be a member of our supporters' club, obviously, 'cos if you're not there's no benefits for you. Membership is, I think, 29 quid and then we may have to pay for tickets in advance – obviously it's no good if somebody doesn't pay in advance and then doesn't turn up, we're left with the ticket. When we first started in 1996, it was a lot more work because both of us had never done anything like that before, and it was back and forwards to people's houses. Now, luckily, we only live about half a mile apart.'

Of the many contradictions that football supporters exhibit, perhaps the sharpest is the attitude to fans who aren't locals. Fans from outside other clubs' immediate area are objects of ridicule, but fans from outside the catchment area of your own club are a cause of great pride. But why does a down-to-earth Cumbrian choose a club often portrayed as the epitome of Cockney flash?

'I can't put me finger on when I started supporting them exactly, but it would be round about 1970,' says Mally. 'I've got a brother who's three years older than me and the lad he used to knock about with, he was a Spurs fan, so I just kind of followed. I don't know whether it was the name Tottenham Hotspur, it's different from your Uniteds and your Cities.

'Then obviously in the early '70s, the big success with the UEFA Cup and the two League Cups. Me dad was never a football fan, never went to football matches. I left school and started working and earning some money, and that coincided with them going into the Second Division. Then we had Burnley, Blackpool, Blackburn, Sunderland, Oldham: all local to Carlisle. You didn't need a ticket for the game. Go home from work on the Friday, go down to the local station, find out the train timetable, get up on a Saturday morning, jump on a train and go to the game.

'First ever game I can really remember down here was when I came down to watch Leeds United in 1979. We beat them 2–1. I remember Glenn Hoddle scored the winner late on, and the keeper at the time for Leeds, he says: "Well, we kept them out, but when somebody like him gets on the ball, what do you do? He can do anything with the ball."

'First ever game I saw them live, we played Carlisle in 1972. We played Carlisle twice within about two years. One was the League Cup, we won 3–1 at Carlisle. I'm sure Chivers scored a couple that night. And then the FA Cup game, we beat them 3–2. I was 12 years old, something like that.

'I started following them really in 1977–78 when we went down, started work and then got married in '81. Once you have kids – I've got two – you just can't afford to go to the games, and then all-ticket games were starting to come in so it was a lot more difficult to get a ticket for the game and everything, so I went a long time without seeing them. I went to all the cup finals early '80s and the UEFA Cup final '84 and did the Cup final '87, and there was sort of one-off games, but I didn't start following them again till about 1994–95.'

Tommy made what seems an even more unlikely choice, coming

as he does from Newcastle, where some would have you believe support for the local United is a condition of residency.

'I've been interested in Spurs since I was eight,' he says. 'When they won the Cup and the Double, we got the wrong Sunday newspapers delivered. We got the *Empire News* instead of the *News of the World*, and there was a big cover picture which went up on me bedroom wall just 'cos I was starting to get interested in football. And me dad says, "Ah, they're a good team, they're a good side," and then he kept going on about Jimmy Greaves. And I says to him, "Who is this Jimmy Greaves?" and he says, "I'll take you to Newcastle", so that was the first live game I saw. We won 2–0 and that was the October 1965 game at St James's Park; there were 54,000 there. I vividly remember this because I was up at the terraces with me dad and couldn't really see, and all these Geordie blokes lifted us up so that I could get a better look. Then I was hooked like, that was it.

'There was a group of lads at school that were Spurs fans, some were Liverpool. We used to go down to home games and 'cos me dad worked on the railway I could go for nothing for three journeys and then a quarter fare for the rest. But you used to have to leave at two o'clock in the morning, get an early train, as they were all diesels, and it used to take about six or seven hours to get to London. Then you were in London, but you couldn't get a later train 'cos you couldn't make the kick-off. A bit like now really [laughs].'

Mally and Tommy also undermine the misconception among some people that the game is now watched solely by middle-class professionals.

'I'm a pipe fitter/welder by trade,' says Mally. 'I work in the local biscuit factory for a bit of overtime, which pays for my football, so obviously the Sunday games you have to pick and choose, with Sky getting involved. I couldn't do Leicester last week 'cos we had Middlesbrough this week – you have to make these sacrifices to be able to go to the games.'

Televised football is held up as a great provider, usually by TV companies, but the claims fall on stony ground for committed fans like Mally and Tommy.

'TV makes it a nightmare for us,' says Mally. 'We have to organise trips, and sometimes there could be 40 or 50, and trying to organise that and the game getting changed six weeks beforehand or even closer than that . . . We've organised tickets, organised travel, then next minute somebody can't go 'cos the game's changed, you're taking tickets back to the office . . . It's an absolute nightmare sometimes.

'But I'd rather travel down. Even though it's a long day out, I don't think there's any substitute for watching the game live. You meet friends that we've made over the years and see them in the pub before the game, have a bit of banter with them and a bit of a craic and everything. No, there's no substitute.'

There may be no substitute for a live game, but displays like the one against Middlesbrough are a poor substitute for what most fans expect, let alone those who've gone to the effort and expense Mally and Tommy have.

'I've said many a time, why do we put the effort in?' says Tommy. 'I work full time as a fabricator and a welder. I do at least 46 hours a week doing that and then I have a little job at the local newspaper – that pays for my football, that gets me away to matches. You get up four or five in the morning; it can be up to an 18-hour day, which is a long day to see 90 minutes of football.

'One prime example, we went to Bradford, which is not that far, that was one of the shorter days. And Tim Sherwood turned up, got off the bus, put the shirt on and that's all he did. He did nothing. As I say, you do these long days and you can see the effort's not there. You think, why did we bother?

'But I suppose in a way, it's like a bit of a drug, isn't it? You need a fix. I'd rather go to a game that they'd lost than sit at home when they got beat. I'm more depressed if I've sat at home, 'cos you read the newspapers the next day, they've hit the bar, they've hit the post, you think God, we should've won that game. But the true reflection of the game, which you only get if you're there, you can see they got beat fair and square, there's no excuses. It's not so bad if they put an effort in.'

Mally and Tommy provide yet another example of how the 'fickle' label applied to Spurs fans is misguided. What is beyond doubt is that Spurs fans are never slow to let their feelings be known. So what do Mally and Tommy think of the various fans' groups that have sprung up at Tottenham, and do they think the fans should have a more formal voice?

Tommy's blunt about it. 'They're quite happy to take yer money, so why shouldn't fans have an input? They too often think supporters are fools, but there's a lot of wise people who come here week in and week out.'

'The club's trying to portray this image that they'd like the fans to have an input,' says Mally, 'but I think at the end of the day they don't really give a damn. And it's their reputations. You've got Daniel Levy, is he going to let somebody off the street influence his decisions? Yeah, he'll hold meetings and say he listens, but I don't think at the end of the day it makes a hap'orth of difference. But you need fans to voice an opinion.'

So what can Spurs achieve when, or if, they ever get it right? The duo's answers could be seen as examples of the limited ambitions of many fans of clubs outside the modern big three, or just as painfully realistic. What's pretty certain is that they wouldn't have said this 20 years ago.

'I can't see us winning the Championship,' says Mally. 'You've got the Man Uniteds, Arsenal, Chelsea now with all the money, then there's half a dozen clubs fighting for those three European places.

'We've got to start qualifying for Europe every year. If we get to the Champions League, that would be a bonus. You'll have yer Southamptons and Blackburns doing it once every five years, but the likes of Tottenham should be doing it every year. I'd hope we can make that next step.

'My ambition is to watch 'em in Europe. Last time we were in Europe coincided with us going to America, and in the early '80s it wasn't as easy to travel, especially from Carlisle. But now, with the EasyJets and what have you, it's probably cheaper to watch 'em in Europe than travel down here.'

Making that next step up, it's generally agreed, means getting more fans in regularly to help finance a push on to the next level. But how to do this would be the subject of much controversy as the season wore on. Perhaps surprisingly, Mally and Tommy have a keen sense of where home is, despite coming from so far away from 'the world famous home of the Spurs'.

'We need to do something with the ground,' says Mally. 'Travelling about these past few seasons, the new grounds, Middlesbrough, Bolton, Derby, Leicester – if you close yer eyes, turn around three times and open yer eyes up, you could be in any one of them grounds. And I would hate that to happen to us. You go to Anfield, there's something about it. The old Kop's gone and it's not the same, but it's still got the history, there's something about it. I'd hate us to move.

'There's enough scope there. They talk about these transport issues, to me that's just excuses. You get people from all over the country, all over Europe travelling here, and they don't think, "Oh, we need another Tube stop." They come here [anyway]. I think it's a bargaining tool they're trying to use against the council.'

Mally's also got some very strong views on one option the club keep attempting to fly. 'There's no way on earth, if they're Tottenham fans like they say they are, that they'd share a ground with Arsenal,' he says.

But enough of the off-field wrangles, it's what happens on the pitch that counts. With their long record of support, who's the best player either man has seen?

'Greaves,' says Tommy right away. 'His record speaks for itself. He scored 44 goals for England in 57 appearances. Goal-scoring-wise, he was the best, but as a footballer he was lazy, he'll admit that. I've read every book there is to read about Greaves and he says it in all of them. He says he hated training. His pre-match meal with Terry Venables was pie and mash in Canning Town. But for pure goal-scoring ability, he can't be touched.'

Mally's choice is Hoddle. 'What he could do with a football was absolutely amazing. I played football from when I left school to me late 30s and what he could do . . . Obviously we're all kids at heart and you try to emulate him on a football pitch and you think, "How does he do that?" He could totally change a game: that season that we had Garth Crooks and Steve Archibald playing in the early '80s – he said they were a dream to play for, he knew he could look up and play a 40-yard ball, spot on, amazing. Me other was Steve Perryman, he was Tottenham through and through, and probably his downfall was when he just started off in the club. He was just so pleased to be in the team he'd play in any position, instead of saying hang on a minute, I want to play right-back. They reckon him and Billy Bonds were the best uncapped players.'

In all the years of following Spurs, there must have been some memorable trips, and Mally closes with the tale of two crackers.

'There was one game in our promotion year, 1978, away to

Southampton, last game of the season. I left Carlisle at 8.30 on the Friday morning and caught a train to Southampton, arriving there at 4.30 p.m. I stayed at my mate's relations' house; they'd got me a ticket for the game in the home end as I couldn't get one through Spurs. We went out for a drink on the Friday night and all the pubs had signs outside saying, "No trainers, no jeans, no Spurs fans", as coaches were arriving and just dropping people off, then heading back to London.

'I arrived at the ground early on the Saturday and a steward let me into the Spurs end. At the end of the game I managed to get on to the pitch along with another few thousand Spurs fans to celebrate promotion. I can't remember much about the game, only they hit the post in the last few minutes. On Saturday night we sank a few beers and had a good knees-up down the local pub and the locals couldn't believe we had travelled so far to see a game of football. Sunday morning we left Southampton at 10 a.m., arriving back in Carlisle late evening, complete with a most enjoyable hangover. I wish we could have more trips like that.

'Another memorable trip we did was in 1984 for the UEFA Cup final v. Anderlecht. I remember how quiet the streets and pubs were, so we decided to go straight into the ground. As the game was pay on the turnstiles, no ticket required, everyone had the same idea and the atmosphere before kick-off was fantastic. We stood on the Shelf that night and I can't remember it ever being so crammed full at a football match.

'Anyway, the game is history now and because it went into extra time we had a rush to catch our train. We waited until the cup was presented then ran all the way to Seven Sisters, got the Tube, ran up the escalators, down the platform . . . only to see our train just pulling away from the platform. So we caught a train to Crewe, waited in the buffet there for four hours, got a train to Preston, waited there for another hour and finally caught the Glasgow train, getting off at Carlisle at 10.30 a.m., Thursday. Did we get some funny looks walking out of Carlisle station at that time of morning, covered in Spurs colours, singing "We won the Cup".

'That were just another 24-hour trip in the life of a Cumbria Spurs fan. I hope them days will soon return.'

4

We will fight forever more: 'Paul'

Hark now hear the Tottenham sing
The Arsenal run away
And we will fight forever more
Because of Boxing Day

For the final game in October, a derby against West Ham in the Carling Cup, Spurs would have to put in a much better effort. But the first full house of the season saw both sides grind out a goalless 90 minutes before, in extra time, Bobby Zamora bagged his first goal for the club to send the Hammers out. It wasn't inspiring, but Spurs were making progress.

The tie also brought more unwelcome publicity off the pitch after a serious outbreak of crowd trouble before the game. At about 4 p.m., a mob of around 100 West Ham fans had attacked the pub in the High Road where many of Tottenham's faces were known to drink and wrecked it. The police struggled to contain hand-to-hand fighting in the street, and there was widespread traffic chaos as roads were blocked off to quell the riot. The remaining hours before kick-off at 7.45 p.m. simmered, with the police out in force but unable to prevent two more pubs being wrecked as mobs of Spurs and West Ham hooligans hunted each other through the streets. Such a major incident so close to a ground was unusual. Some saw an effort by West Ham's infamous Inter City Firm (ICF) to put down a marker that, despite their club's relegation, they were still a force to be reckoned with.

The incidents also showed how Tottenham's hooligan tendency was very much alive and kicking, just as at many other clubs. Unlike many other clubs, however, that particular kind of following appears to be growing in profile and confidence at Spurs. Just ask Paul, a dyed-in-the-wool fan who, in the right circumstances, is also prepared literally to fight for the Tottenham cause, a belief he expresses with a blunt statement of intent.

'We don't run. In my experience, I've never seen a modern-day Tottenham firm run from Arsenal, never seen them run from Chelsea, though, to be honest with you, Arsenal are a fucking joke. I think that's because of their success. The more successful a club becomes, the more they lose track of the hooligan thing. They're doing their stuff on the pitch, so what do they want notoriety off it for?

'What have we got? We've got nothing on the pitch, so if we want notoriety and want to brag, we have to find it in other forms. We want to be top firm because we're not known for anything else. And I tell you now, Tottenham *are* known; we're known at away games because we're all game boys. And we don't run. Simple.'

Paul is in his early 30s, a second-generation member of an immigrant community, born and bred in north London, and with a good job in the City. By his own frequent admission, he is not an out-and-out hooligan – 'I'm small scale' – but he is one of many supporters willing to defend what they perceive as the club's honour: if necessary by means of direct physical confrontation with rival fans.

Paul chooses his words carefully and is keen at all times to preserve his own anonymity. 'Paul' is not his real name: the material risks that come with exposure mean he is understandably reluctant to give too much away.

What he does describe is a world of football far removed from the cheery picture of beaming families kitted out in official club merchandise, dutifully supporting their club in mute, well-behaved conformity. Paul describes a world of fights, booze- and drug-fuelled adventures home and abroad in the company of a rogue's gallery of colourful and occasionally fearsome characters, all in the name of following Spurs. At times it's a richly funny scene, at others a depressingly violent one.

There will be people reading this, other contributors to this book among them, who will be appalled that we have given such a story any exposure. Indeed, the growth of football hooliganism literature means that the tales of aggro have a wearingly familiar ring to them. Not for nothing has it been described as 'hooligan porn'.

To ignore this aspect of Tottenham's support, however, would be to neglect a crucial component of the club's modern character. There are hundreds of Spurs fans prepared to get physically involved, should the situation arise. Perhaps thousands more have an interest in what goes on. Many will never throw a punch in football anger in their life, but they will bask in the reflected glory; others will despair at the reputation the violence earns for the club. Like it or loathe it, the reality is that hooliganism continues to be a fact of football life and, by common consent in hooligan circles, Tottenham's various crews now together constitute one of the top firms in the country.

It is worth taking any report of hooliganism with a large pinch of salt; such activities may be the result more of feverish imaginations, dreamed up by nice suburban boys from the comfort of their own computers, rather than actual reality. Paul, however, experiences the real thing. He is wary of divulging specific names, holding to an unwritten agreement between those genuinely in the know who like to keep certain things to themselves.

'What you've got with Tottenham is lots of little firms,' Paul explains. 'If you want to call my little lot a firm, then what you've got is a collective of little firms. With other clubs you've got big collectives like the ICF, the Bushwhackers, etc. With Spurs it's all little firms, but I tell you what: on their day when they all get together and unite – we're fucking invincible.

'It's not so much names of firms, it's that a lot of them are run by geezers and you know them by the fella's name – so-and-so's firm, so-and-so's mob, and there's plenty of them about. You know who they are, they know who you are.'

Paul is known, having devoted years to following the club at home and abroad. Primarily, he is a fan, but in certain circumstances he is prepared to muck in. 'I've never really been affiliated to an organised firm as such. I knock about with a bunch of game boys. There's a good dozen of us, I'm pretty well known at away games amongst the Spurs following. I go to 75 per cent of the away games, and you get to know all the fellas on the circuit.

'But organised stuff? I've never picked up the phone and arranged to have a knuckle with another firm. I've had plenty of knuckles with plenty of firms because we're in the wrong place at the wrong time.

'The best way to describe it is that the lads I meet up with at every game, at home as well, we don't run. If it's there and it happens, I'm more than happy to jump in, right? Because what I don't want to see is one of my mates getting spanked, or them watching me getting spanked. But that don't happen.'

By way of example, he cites a game at Craven Cottage a couple of years ago. 'You don't really associate Fulham with a firm, but every club's got a few nutters. One of these turns round to my mate and says, "If you want it, let's have it now in Bishop's Park." So this Fulham bloke's gone bosh and hit this Spurs fan. It all goes off and it gets a bit hairy; through no choice I've had to throw a few punches.

'It turns out my best mate sees a bloke taking a right fucking hiding. And it turns out that this bloke has got exactly the same coat as me, so he thought it was me. He got hold of these two traffic cones and he started waving 'em like fucking John Wayne with a lasso. He must have taken about eight of them out by himself. And he's taken his belt off and with the buckle he's fucking lumping every cunt he can find. He didn't know it weren't me taking that kicking but he was prepared to go in there, on his Jack Jones.

'I knock about with guys that come from all sorts of walks of life. Not all of them are from London, and that's the beauty of it – we are Spurs united. It don't matter where you're from or how you talk, if you're Tottenham, you're Tottenham, and we all look after each other.'

Paul and his friends are just as dedicated to the club, with a strong sense of local identity.

'Wherever fans come from, that's the magnet – Tottenham Hotspur, Tottenham the area. I tell you now, all this bollocks about merging a stadium with Arsenal and sharing Wembley, I will not be a season-ticket holder any more. I'll always love the club, but, at the end of the day, it's where we're from. It just so happens that that area has got a football club that we've all got an affinity with, a bond, and something we can regard as our own. Tottenham's a shithole, but it's our shithole.'

Any perceived insult against the club and that sense of local identity is likely to inspire the same kind of attitude as any slight – physical or otherwise – against individuals. It's this belief that strikes at the heart of what turns Paul and his mates from being dedicated fans to what the public regards as 'hooligans'.

'What we don't like is some other firm coming and make cunts out of us in our own backyard. If that's going to happen, then they are going to know about it. A couple of seasons ago, we drew Cardiff in the Cup. They came down midweek, Spurs could spot 'em a mile off 'cos they're stupid fucking dumb Taffs wearing Burberry and Aquascutum, so they're just like a walking advert for saying, "Give me a good knuckle."

'They brought, what, a few thousand? And they thought, "Midweek, we'll come and take the piss." What happened was that Tottenham grouped and that was it. Fair play to them, they put on a good show but they were sent packing with a big, big flea up their arse. They were coming along the High Road in minibuses with Welsh placenames on them, and Spurs were just kicking the fuck out of them. They came; they went.

'The point I'm trying to make is this: I'm not a hooligan, but it's an honour thing with me, it's about someone taking the piss. You ain't going to allow someone to do that in your own home, and you ain't going to allow someone to do that in Tottenham, because Tottenham is your home. It's what we are.

'Take Chelsea a few years back. Word had got around that they were bringing down a bit of a firm for an FA Cup game. We come out of the pub and we were just edging along the High Road when we saw a very, very notorious, very naughty Tottenham firm. They've clocked us, we've clocked them, we know who they are, and we start having a bit of a chat.

'Then, about six or seven Chelsea geezers start appearing and start to walk through. Now they must have been bouncers. They were fucking massive, all wearing long leather coats, proper doormen, no one shorter than 6 ft 3 in. tall, proper lumps – bruisers.

'I saw them moving towards us, talking to each other. One of them turned and he must have said to the rest of them, "We're walking into a Spurs firm here." Nothing was discussed, but you just knew that you weren't going to let them just walk through you. If they'd have walked through you, they would have gone back to their fucking Fulham Road or wherever it is they come from and given it the biggun about walking through our main firm – which I'm not part of, you understand, but I was with at that part of the day – and us doing fuck all. It weren't going to happen.

'They carried on walking and one of them did like a kind of snort, as if to say, "We're walking through your firm, and you've done fuck all." So one of my mates lobbed a bottle at 'em. Now, these geezers were waiting to have an off, and I've got to admit they were game boys. There was only a handful of them, there was a good 20 of us, but we didn't all jump in; we made the numbers "fair". One of them has turned around, swung a punch, and he's caught another mate square on the face. This mate of mine is a game boy, in his 40s, and he's been floored.

'Now one of my best pals he's about 5 ft 7 in. tall, not a big fella, but I will never forget this till the day I die: he launched a punch from the ground with all the might his mother gave birth to him with, and he's hit this Chelsea geezer and I've heard his fucking face go crack. One punch, and he just collapsed on the floor. Then about five or six geezers piled into him, more of them came over, and then they took a good hiding. But fair play to Chelsea – they stood there for the knuckle.'

It's a common-enough tale and could be written about any number of fans from any number of clubs. Paul's story is different, though.

To begin with, he is in some respects an unlikely Spurs fan. Traditionally members of Paul's community have tended to follow Arsenal. Settling in Islington, Finsbury Park and Kentish Town from the early 1960s, those immigrants gravitated towards Highbury. As their communities have spread out to other north London areas, so many among the second generation began to support Spurs, but Paul could easily have become a supporter fighting for the Arsenal cause.

'When I was a kid, the onus was on me to follow Arsenal and not Tottenham. My dad owned a working-man's caff in Islington, where I used to help out. All the workmen there used to support Arsenal and ask me who I supported. I would say, with pride, "Tottenham." They would give me all sorts of grief, but there was just something I enjoyed about being the underdog.

'Ever since I can remember, I've always followed football and followed Tottenham; where I grew up it was either Spurs or Arsenal. My cousin is a big West Ham fan, and I suppose I've always looked up to him. He used to run with one of their firms at one point, but even though he pushed me towards West Ham, it was at the time when Spurs were playing good football. The way Spurs played, the class, everything, they were just that little bit more glamorous. So that's how it all started.'

His first game in 1979, a home win against Notts Forest secured through a Glenn Hoddle special, cemented that bond. 'I really remember distinctly from that game my disappointment at how small the ground was. When you see it on *Match of the Day* with the wide lens, it looked so much bigger. But I loved the atmosphere on the terracing, the way the ground shook, the surges. I remember when the game got started, there was beer being slung all over the place and I got drenched. I went home stinking of it. It was great; didn't see much of it because of my height but just being there was enough. It swept me away.'

His heroes were Hoddle, Chris Hughton and Ossie Ardiles, but, perhaps tellingly, he loved the no-nonsense, all-round effort and commitment of other players like Graham Roberts and Steve Perryman – players prepared to put their foot in for the Spurs cause.

Paul has enjoyed many memorable moments since that time, ranking the winning home leg of the UEFA Cup final in 1984 as the most enjoyable. 'It's one of the most uplifting experiences I've ever had. I knot up just thinking about it.' A couple of years later, things changed. Paul had his first direct experience of trouble, and it marked a turning point in his understanding of being a football supporter.

'It was at West Ham, in the away end at Upton Park. Spurs scored and the whole fucking place erupted. In all this turmoil, this Tottenham fan's turned round and lumped this copper and he's gone down. The copper gets up and grabs the first bloke he can find, and that's me.

'He's got his truncheon out and started whacking me, and two of his mates have come in and dragged me down the steps. I lost a shoe and they've taken me into the charge room. I must have been about 17, 18. They've gone, "Name?" and I've given them a false one. I knew about what to say from my cousin. I didn't have any ID on me. I was always skint in them days, so I didn't have any cards or anything like that. So I've given them a false name, address, all this bollocks, and they didn't charge me, they just wanted to eject me.

'I'd heard stories that West Ham's Under-5s [the junior branch of West Ham's hooligan element] used to hang around outside the away end, that's how they used to prove themselves by taking on guys, picking them off as they got thrown out of the ground. So I knew what was going to happen, and I turned round to the copper and I said, "You can't throw me out because these Under-5s are going to have me." He said, "You should have fucking thought about that before you decided to pile into my mate." I tried to explain that it wasn't me, but he weren't having it, so they threw me out.

'I admit I was shitting myself. There were about six or seven of these Under-5s outside. They were round the same age, about 18, 19. They've come up to me and said, "We don't know who the fuck you are, you've got a big nose so you must be a fucking Yid," and they start chasing me. What could I do? I don't know the back streets of West Ham. I've jumped over fences until I've jumped over one and it was covered in glass, stuck on top. They've caught up with me, and given me a right fucking turning over, a real bad beating, hospital job. And that's where it all started really, it just built up my hate for fans of other clubs, you know? It made me that bit more wary.'

Not that it put Paul off. 'I got over it, and bruises and black eyes heal. Whilst it didn't make me go in for it, it didn't make me run from it either. That's the way it was drummed into me. We're Spurs and we don't run.'

If this was a typical introduction to hooliganism, it is an experience others have gone through but managed to put behind them without becoming hooligans themselves. But those wishing to conveniently pigeon-hole Paul under a heading marked 'thug' will be disappointed. He counters the notion that hooligans are not fans – this is a man, after all, who has disobeyed the most important of demands for family unity, missing out on celebrations in order to travel to away games. He talks at length about the game, expressing his opinions with a depth of knowledge only the true fanatic can match.

Take this on David Pleat: 'It's a cancer at the club, this Continental style of having a Director of Football. Wherever they've tried it, it's never really worked. Pleat has been the root of a lot of our problems, with personality clashes with Graham and Hoddle, and I think the board are blind because they are solely guided by this one man.

'Whoever's implemented the policy of bringing through youth, and by some accounts that is Pleat, that's great, but that's only great if we can hold on to them. In the past, not too many came through the ranks. Now we've got a few more, but the current squad is far from good enough to compete. We're inconsistent – we skin a team 3–0 one week and then go and lose 4–0 the next. That's not a good sign. When you're inconsistent, that means you're not a good side. We lack leadership.'

It's articulate views such as these that are at odds with the orthodox image of the football hooligan – the Neanderthal, knuckle-scraping bogeyman of media invention who has no interest in the actual game of football. It is a falsehood that angers Paul.

'I'm not an out-and-out hooligan, right? I'm a fan first and foremost, but it is a myth that hooligans are not fans. They're big-time fans, real die-hards. I know geezers that come from all over England to follow Tottenham, and part of the parcel is that they enjoy a knuckle, but they are staunch fans. And it's not just that they support the club – you can ask them anything about Tottenham – statistics, what was the score in 1975 against blah, blah, blah? – whatever, these geezers will know. They know their history of the badge, the area, the ground, everything.

'This inaccurate image does wind me up. All right, some headbangers are mindless and they should know better, but I think a lot of them are driven to fight because of their passion for the club – they don't want to get the piss taken out of their club. Results matter. If you get spanked three fucking nil by Chelsea, you ain't going to walk out of that stadium and let them spank you outside of the ground as well. Then again, if you spank Chelsea 3–0, a rare occurrence these days, you want to go outside and carry it on: "Fuck you, we done you on the pitch, we'll have the Double over you today. We'll do you outside as well."'

Paul's opinions reflect his belief of how supporters in general are treated badly by their clubs. As someone who spends a large proportion of his income and time on supporting Tottenham, he is enraged by this seemingly contemptuous attitude, and how the nature of the support has altered.

'The way clubs are run now is poor – the lack of cooperation when you ring up the ticket office, for example. They run it as a business and they have to, but there's far too much emphasis on money.

'All you hear is Tottenham fans fucking moaning, and it's all 'cos we're not producing, but the new breed, I'm appalled. They don't even know the songs any more. They look at you and think you're from the planet Mars. We're a dying breed, man. But clubs don't want the old-style fan any more. They want the new-style corporate customer. They're not bothered about the guy that struggles with his £600-a-year season ticket that he has to pay off every month 'cos he's skint. We're the people who buy the merchandise and the shirts. Why don't they give fans testimonials? Why for every ten years that I've had a season ticket can't I have one for free?'

Paul rejects the option of joining supporter organisations as a means to address such discontent. He was briefly a member of one group in the aftermath of the Venables sacking in 1993, but it's results that matter and they are the focus for much of his grievance.

'We've had too many years of hurt. If it means sacrificing the flair – which we haven't been seeing much of lately in any case – then I think enough is enough, the time has come to start winning pots. If that means changing our game a bit, then so be it, because I want to hold my head up high when I come in to work. I get Gooners and Chelsea fans on a Monday queuing up by my desk to take the piss, geezers who I'd be chinning on a Saturday afternoon, but I can't because I'm at work.'

Again, some will react in disgust at such an attitude. But Paul is disarmingly honest as to the justification or otherwise of hooliganism.

'I can understand how people who hate it feel; it is a cancer on the game, but football hooliganism's been here for donkeys, long before you and me came along, and it's going to be here long after we're gone. It's tribal, it's Anglo-Saxon, it's, oh I dunno, the Viking fucking spirit or whatever. We live in a violent society. You've got a lot of men, young and old, who are frustrated, whether they're underachievers or even overachievers, it don't matter – they all want that little something by which they can let off steam.

'So, what I say to these people is, yeah, it ain't right – it's pretty sick to be honest – but that's the way it is. Not everything in life is right – Jews have been killing Arabs, Greeks have been killing Turks, British the Irish and vice versa for centuries. This is just something that, whilst it ain't right, it's part of life. You can take it or leave it.

'Nine times out of ten, there is *some* honour with hooligans and troublemakers; they don't go round lumping shirts, people that don't want to be hit – most of them. They tend to leave Joe Public alone. I've seen a couple of Tottenham boys hit shirts and their own firm turn on them. There is *some* honour in a sick sort of way. It's not right. You could even describe it as cowardice, because it's hunting in packs. There's very few geezers who are just going to rush 20 other geezers.

'So, why do I sometimes get involved? It's a little bit of a buzz. Look, I've got a good job with decent prospects, but at the end of the day – and I'm not saying this is right – I'm taking shit from someone nine to five on a daily basis; I can't answer him back, I can't really say too much to him. So on a Saturday afternoon, it's my turn to go out, have a few bevvies and give someone else a bit of fucking grief, if that's what he wants.

'I often say to myself, "I ain't doing that again – that's fucking out of order, I've hurt that geezer." But it's that pride thing again: you can't let geezers take the piss. Because their mentality hasn't changed. Yours might, but theirs won't, and they'll still come and take liberties.'

Paul has witnessed first hand arguably the ugliest side of this mentality – England fans abroad. His brief period of support for the national side brought him into contact with a varied bunch of people and some eventful experiences. There was the ex-pat he met in Sweden whose wife thought he was working as a labourer in Germany, when he was, in fact, a 'fluffer' – a warm-up man for female porn actresses. 'Ugly fucker, though, terrible teeth, probably couldn't take a leading role for obvious reasons.'

Then there was the time in a Luxembourg brothel. It was packed with England fans totally disinterested in the entertainment on offer, there because it was the only place serving alcohol to visiting supporters. 'All they wanted was the beer. We got slung out in the end, arrested and banged up at the airport after some coppers came in and found a bit of blow on a fan. We were in the wrong place at the wrong time – the reputation had preceded us.'

That reputation, however, is undoubtedly deserved. Because of his ethnic background, Paul was an unlikely England fan, shunned by many other England followers.

'I've always had a passion for England, but I've never forgot my roots. A lot of mates think I've got a bit of a split personality: I can be the most traditional family bloke you can imagine and then in a blink I'm "England my England". However, I never really got any respect when I went to England games because I've got the foreign name on the British passport. I look different to your average England fan, and I used to get comments – "You fucking wog" sort of thing – and I never really felt part of the England family.

'Now? I'm not that bothered; I don't want to know. The team are sub-standard and some of the fans let them down. Some are mindless, some are idiots, and because of their ignorance they don't embrace all England fans. There's never that camaraderie you get with Spurs.

'Some England fans have got different agendas. At the end of the day, I say fuck all that; those days are behind me. I've seen it and don't want a part of it. I've been to Poland and been in a bar and there's geezers there who probably can't even spell their own names boasting about how they'd been to Auschwitz and pissed on the graves. They don't even know the history of the place, how Jewish people were persecuted. They're just bigots. They appal me. People might think that's a bit rich coming from me, but I do have standards. I'm an educated bloke, and I know about peoples' histories, but they disrespect everyone.'

There is another group that he dislikes – players. Most fans become cynical as they grow older, when it becomes plain that their heroes are in reality unremarkable individuals uninterested in their own supporters. Paul has direct experience, based on a pre-season friendly in the Netherlands a few years ago.

'On the trip home, we got to the departure lounge and we happened to be on the same flight as the players. In the lounge, sprawled out with his legs across the aisle was a very famous Tottenham footballer at the time, someone who was never too popular. I couldn't get through because of his legs, and I was loaded down with my bag and couldn't jump over. He's only got to think, "Hang on, these boys have come all this way, they're Tottenham, just give them a bit of courtesy." But he's looked at me and he's gone, "What?" I bit it. I said, "I tell you *what*, why don't you just move your fucking legs out the way? You've seen me coming and any decent polite human being, never mind a footballer, would have moved his legs."

'He just said to me, "Go over them." I said, "I tell you what, mate, why don't I do us all a favour and instead of going over them, just snap your fucking shins, put you out of your misery 'cos you're a shit footballer, and, in the meantime, it might teach you a few manners." Straight away, this other very famous footballer at Tottenham has piped up and gone to defend him. I turned to him and said, "And as for you, with the amount of injuries you've had, if you were a horse they'd have fucking shot you by now, you cunt." So all his mates started laughing and taking the piss, and on the flight home all the squad were just making these neighing horse noises!

'I've got no time for them. As a youngster, I used to stick up for players like Hoddle and Ardiles if they were getting stick from other fans, to the extent that I'd have a knuckle over it – but not any more. I don't give a shit about them.

'They'd be stupid for turning down the money they're offered, so I blame the clubs a bit. I don't mean to be disrespectful, but footballers are not the most intelligent people. Some are, some aren't; most of the ones I've met aren't. When you throw someone into the limelight and you give him £20k a week, fast car, fast bird and everyone's making a big deal about it, then he's bound to go off the rails. Maybe the clubs are not helping them and coaching them the way they should. Because at the end of the day, they are ambassadors for the world's game. These people are role models, but, to be honest, I wouldn't piss on them if they was on fire. Young upstarts like Bowyer: to be honest, if Bowyer was in here now, I'd probably knock him out. I'd just chin him. If he walked into a pub in Tottenham, he'd soon get it, I can tell you.'

Paul is incensed by players' more extreme behaviour, particularly after the 2003–04 season when so many accusations of rape were levelled against individuals.

'The greed of footballers and the way they carry on off the pitch disgusts me. I haven't got any kids, but I will have one day, and the way some players are going out, doing the drugs, spit roasting and gang raping, or whatever it is they fucking do, I mean, they are supposed to be role models. These people should know better. They are in the spotlight, in the public eye, and they should behave better. My kids, one day, may be looking up to these wankers. They appal me.'

It is a moral stance perhaps at odds with the behaviour of many of Paul's fellow fans; indeed, a contradiction given his own willingness to indulge in the kind of activity that shocks 'ordinary' fans. Paul makes no apologies. What he gets up to is largely his own concern and that of like-minded people – all is fair in love and war, perhaps, when you make such an effort supporting Tottenham. And there have been plenty of laughs along the way.

'Me and one of my best pals went to Notts Forest in the League Cup a few years back. It was a Sunday game and it was when there was still standing at the City Ground, with no cover. It was pissing down with rain that day, really pouring. I think we won 1–0, but we got absolutely soaked. In those days, I had a dodgy Mk IV Cortina, that was our away-match travel. We were just so cold and so wet, I had this flash of genius to get all our kit off and try and get a bit dry and warm in the car. So you had these two geezers in this Cortina, with just our trainers and our pants on.

'We were on the motorway heading back to London when we see this blue light and we get pulled. These two coppers come up, and you can just picture the scene – there's us two sitting there virtually stark bollock naked and this copper looks a bit bemused and says to us, "What are you doing?" I said to him, "We're a bit wet, so we put the gear in the back and turned the heaters up, otherwise we were going to die of pneumonia." They weren't having it and told us to put our gear on, otherwise they were going to arrest us for public indecency or causing an accident.

'In fact, Notts Forest hasn't been lucky for me. There was the time up there with my mate Billy the Dog, who liked a bit of charlie. I drove up there, and then he was supposed to drive us back 'cos I'd had a few beers. But it starts snowing, a real blizzard, the game's called off and Billy's got to try and drive us home. He's high as a kite, thinks the snow is hilarious and wants to get out and sniff it all.

'On top of that, Billy the Dog's lost control of the car and smashed my motor up in the central reservation. To make it even worse, the windscreen wipers have packed up – so every now and then, I'm having to lean out through the sunroof as we're going along with a Spurs scarf trying to clear the windscreen. All the while he's laughing like mad. It took us nine hours to get back.

'You meet some real characters. When we played Vitesse Arnhem in a pre-season friendly, me and a few geezers went and on the way out there at the airport we bumped into this geezer we'll call Big Terry. He's a proper fucking spiv, always brings a few boys with him, but he's a likeable rogue, a bit like Fagin – anything for a buck. They delayed a couple of flights that his boys would have been on because they've overbooked or something. So he went up to the desk to sort it out, and I've heard him doing a deal, asking for compensation, and they've said that for every man on the flight they'll give £65.

'He had about 25 geezers booked on the flight so he held back about 15 of them and he's given a load of bullshit and gone, "It's not good, lads – they've double-booked, but I've negotiated a good deal, boys. You're going on the next flight in an hour and a half, plus you're all going to get £30 compensation."

'Anyway, we've had a right good laugh on the trip. All got puffed up on this train going to the game, and this geezer has got a bag of mushrooms, so we're all high as kites and there's fuck all the Old Bill can do with this train of 400 stoned Spurs fans. We had a great time in Amsterdam.

'It was like when we went to Warrington, the semi-final in 1999 against Newcastle. We've gone down into the town that night and ended up in what is apparently Warrington's most notorious pub. There was 15 of us, so no one was going to fuck around with us. We're all on the beer, a few on the pills, a bit of puff and that, all getting very merry. All of a sudden, my mate says, "You ain't going to believe this – we're in a swingers' pub." Before we knew it, this bird has stuck her tits right in a mate's face and gone, "Have a suck on these."

'Anyway, this geezer keeps on coming up to me saying, "Do you like my missus?" I didn't know what to make of it. Anyway, these birds are all over us, doing God knows what. This fella, Ken his name was, says, "There's plenty more where this come from," and he told us to go down to this club.

'So, we get in this club, and, sure enough, it all gets a bit interesting. This bird comes and sits between me and my mate, and says in a real strong northern accent, "Yer all right, loves, fancy going skiing?" and starts wanking the pair of us off. There's a mate having it away with another one on the dance floor and this geezer Ken is buying us drinks all night. Mad.

'Two years later we're up in Warrington for the semi against Arsenal. We're in a boozer and one of us spots that it's full of Gooners upstairs. There's a few of us saying, "There's no way we're drinking in a club with a load of Gooners." So, I've gone upstairs and they thought I was a Gooner, so I'm playing along with it and I says to them, "They've got a right fucking firm of Tottenham downstairs. I've heard them going on about how they're going to chin a load of Gooners, do fuck knows what to them. If I was you, I wouldn't go downstairs. In fact, I'd fuck off." So they've gone, "Cheers for the heads up," and they've fucked off out of it. Typical Gooners, they shit their load.

'It's all part of the craic, the camaraderie. Part of the parcel. All in the name of following Spurs.'

5

One team in London: Tunde Banjoko

One team in London
There's only one team in London

At the beginning of November, the third of what had looked like three very winnable home games in a week came with the visit of Bolton, but David Pleat's unbeaten record was ended as Jay-Jay Okocha inspired the visitors to a 1–0 victory. Once more the White Hart Lane PA was turned up to 'very loud' in order to drown out the boos at the final whistle.

David Pleat had lost some sympathy among the fans with his attack on Glenn Hoddle, and now questions were being asked about his selections. With Freddie Kanouté injured, Spurs just couldn't score, and with Gus Poyet and Darren Anderton in central midfield, Spurs could not take hold of a game. And while Pleat also seemed to have brought promising youngster Jonathan Blondel back in from the exile Hoddle had imposed on him, he seemed to be freezing out Rohan Ricketts, a youngster who had impressed when selected by Hoddle. All in all, a game against an unbeaten, table-topping Arsenal was the last thing Spurs needed. But the north London derby, at Highbury, was next.

In recent years, the derby has changed, as the gulf between the two clubs has grown and as local rivalry has turned to bitter hatred for too many fans. Sol Campbell's controversial defection made a bad situation worse, although a growing number of Spurs fans were voicing their annoyance that the favourite chant of the faithful often seemed to be 'Stand up if you hate Arsenal.' In contrast, Arsenal fans liked to affect indifference, but local pride still matters to all who are connected with these two clubs.

In the run-up to the game, a humiliating Spurs defeat was being widely predicted, and some Spurs fans were openly saying that losing by less than two goals would be a result. However, as so often happens, the game threw up the unexpected. In an atmosphere that seemed less poisonous than usual, Spurs took the lead within five minutes, with an even more unlikely detail being the name of the goal-scorer – Darren Anderton. For 60 minutes, Spurs contained and outplayed Arsenal, with young Anthony Gardner keeping superstar Thierry Henry firmly in his pocket. The away support played their part too, roaring their team on and taunting their neighbours with chants of 'Champions League? You're having a laugh.'

Nonetheless, the gnawing feeling that Spurs wouldn't be able to hold on had been growing. Helder Postiga, still looking for his first goal, had fluffed two golden opportunities to put Spurs further ahead in the first half and now, as the seconds ticked away, Arsenal brought on Dennis Bergkamp – so often the scourge of Tottenham in these games. The threat to Tottenham's goal grew until an equaliser came, albeit one inspired by a suspiciously offside-looking Henry. Then, with ten minutes to go, a Freddie Ljungberg shot took a huge deflection off Stephen Carr and Arsenal had won.

Spurs had performed much, much better than in the previous three games. Pride was restored and the 'Lucky Arsenal' tag that so infuriates Gooners was being dusted off by the press post-match. But Spurs were dropping points and nearing the wrong end of the table. Had things become so bad that losing to Arsenal was seen as a kind of victory?

One fan who thinks there is something very wrong with that attitude is Tunde Banjoko, who articulated the feelings of a growing number of Spurs fans in the days following the derby.

'I've got nothing but praise for Tottenham supporters, particularly some of our away supporters,' he says. 'But what pisses me off, quite frankly, is the amount of "Stand up if you hate Arsenal" chants. I'd much rather hear "Stand up if you love Tottenham." We came out of that game at the weekend and the fans were happy that we didn't get battered three or four nil, as if it's some kind of moral victory. I can't be satisfied with that. We need to get a bit of perspective.'

Perspective is never in short supply when talking to Tunde. Now

40, he's been following Spurs since he was a kid, and combines the quick wit and robust debating style of a native Londoner with the cool overview which stands him in good stead as the manager of an employment project in north-west London. Listening to him talk about the club's efforts to find a manager, you wonder, not for the first time, why it is that clubs don't make more effort to draw on the skills within their fan base. It is a question about whether the Spurs board had been too ready to respond to fan pressure when appointing managers that leads Tunde to give a considered reply.

'I don't think the board particularly knew what they wanted,' he says. 'They went for quick fixes. That's poor management. If I was having problems with a staff member, I would like to think that I would prepare for a time when I was going to have to let them go and already have identified who I wanted to replace them.

'I would take everything into account, like whether that person would be acceptable to the fans – and that's acceptable as opposed to being the fans' darling – and on that criterion I don't think George Graham or Gerry Francis would have got the job. I would check out whether they had a proven track record, I'd check out whether they had an understanding of the current trends in football. I would look to the Continent. I would interview a number of people as well. One of the problems we've had at Spurs is that it seems as if we've gone for one man and that was it. One of the things we've not done, and we must do this time, is ask that candidate what he thinks the problems are and how he would address them. And if that candidate doesn't recognise, for example, something that 36,000 Spurs fans recognise, that we have a problem in central midfield, and if he isn't able to identify people to fill that role, then he should be struck out there and then.

'Without speaking to people and really knowing what their ideas are and how they'd deal with things, how can you know?'

It's not rocket science, but it certainly seems to have been beyond successive Tottenham boards to construct the kind of interview process taken for granted in the real world. Tunde's views on the recent past are also well thought through. So where, in his opinion, did it all go wrong?

'My view is probably not one that a lot of people subscribe to,' he says. 'I think the problem was that [Alan] Sugar got caught up in the wrong thing after his problems with [Terry] Venables. The media depicted Venables as a working-class hero against the evil management, and Sugar concentrated on trying to win that battle as opposed to making sure Spurs were OK.

'I'm glad Venables went. I thought he was a nightmare. I don't think he should have been involved in the business side like he was, and anybody who conducts his affairs like that is not somebody that I hold as a hero, so I'm glad he went. I also had my suspicions about who he picked and why. I know he kept Sol Campbell, but I think he got rid of Chris Fairclough and other black players far too easily.

'I think Sugar got it wrong in his choice of managers. He got rid of Ossie Ardiles possibly a bit too quickly, even though Ossie was having some dodgy results, because the crowd turned against him. He then didn't give Christian Gross a chance. He got [Gerry] Francis in – he was an absolute nightmare. A dour, dour footballer. A man who always seemed to refer to Tottenham in the third person, as opposed to saying "we". He never seemed to ever take on board the fact that he was part of Tottenham. Gross could have been a good manager, but he messed himself up with the way he introduced himself to the Spurs fans, and I think he was on a downer from then on. I thought, even at the time, that he was nowhere near as bad as he was made out to be. He was no Arsène Wenger, though.

'And then [George] Graham – that was a nightmare. Somebody else who had no love for the club and didn't mind showing it. He almost scorned the fans in the club, and I don't think that was ever going to work. He was also a manager whose time had gone. He had done well with Arsenal, but I don't think he was suited to what the Premiership had become. I wanted Graham out after a few months, I'll be honest with you, because I thought his football was poor.

'Then, Glenn Hoddle, who I thought would be the hero. I was glad when he came in, and then at his first signing my heart sank. His first signing, if I'm correct, was to re-sign Les Ferdinand and Darren Anderton. Then there were all these rumours that he was going to get Teddy Sheringham, and I said, "Please don't do that." I'm not one of those to think it was all right for Teddy Sheringham to bugger off to Manchester United, then come back for his pension at Spurs. I wasn't happy with that. But he signed him and he signed Gus Poyet, and I didn't think it was going to work. What we were crying out for at Spurs, I felt, was pace, power and passion. None of those players, in my view, represented all of those [qualities]. I didn't think it was going to work.

'A lot of people got caught up in the fact that we got to the

Worthington Cup final, but what people forget is that that year none of the big sides took the Worthington seriously, none of them, and we had a really easy route towards the final. Our performance in Cardiff, I felt, didn't quite represent some of the stuff I'd seen during the season, and driving back I was disgusted. Disgusted that we didn't perform, disgusted that Glenn insisted on playing old, clapped-out players and not taking them off when they clearly weren't good enough.

'Last season was more of the same. In fact, last season was disgraceful. Last Christmas we lost 4–0 three times on the bounce. It was awful. We'd clearly lost the plot. So basically, I think the problem has been that we haven't got good managers. We've always spent; our spending has always been up there. Sugar has spent his money – even the lot we have now, compared to some, have stuck their hands in their pockets. But the problems are with the managers.

'We are clearly still a big club. In terms of everything – the amount it costs to go to Spurs [laughs], the crowds we get week in week out considering our lack of success. We're a big club; there are no doubts about that in my mind. You go anywhere in the world, still, and they've heard of Tottenham Hotspur. I just don't think we have been shrewd.

'Arsenal are what they are today 'cos of one man – Arsène Wenger. He came in and, I have to be quite honest, I have nothing but admiration for him. He got good players, players who were right for what he needed, players who were athletic, they can get up and down, they were passionate, and he has created what Arsenal is at the moment. If we had got the right manager, we could have had that success.'

Analysing decline seems to be something of a speciality among Spurs fans, and this prompts the question of why so many spend so much time with so little hope. But one of the basic rules is that, once chosen, a team must be stuck with through thick and thin. So what brought Tunde and Tottenham together?

'I can't remember exactly when I started,' he says. 'I know it was before the age of ten – that's thirty-plus years ago. I can't even remember who was in the side but I liked what they stood for. They were a London club and I identified with them. I was a guy from west London, Acton, and so at the time Rangers were a decent side and that's the closest side to me. There's Brentford too, but it was Tottenham – Tottenham all the way. There were no family connections whatsoever. I wouldn't have picked anything up from newspapers because I'm sure I wouldn't have read them at that stage. It would have just been the telly. I was aware they were a big club, a glamorous club, a good club, a great club, and now my loyalty's to them.'

It didn't take long for Tunde to get the live-action bug, and he started going to games at an early age.

'I would have been about 11 or 12 [in the] mid-'70s. I would have jumped on the train at Acton Town, took the Piccadilly line to Green Park and change on to the Victoria line, take that to Seven Sisters and then walk on down Seven Sisters Road. It was a big thing for me then. I was by myself – this tiny little black kid. It's one of the things that I liked, I always felt comfortable. I've been going regularly ever since.

'I spent some time in the Midlands so I would make sure I went to all the games – West Brom, Wolves, Birmingham, Villa – all of them. I used to go to some of the London games as well – West Ham, which was terrifying when I was a youngster. It was good. I just loved being part of something. I enjoyed it greatly.'

While the team is always at the centre of a fan's affections, there are many other details that contribute to the sense of belonging always found in a committed fan. For Tunde, the experiences he had as a black Londoner contributed to the strengthening of his bond with the club.

'These were the days when there weren't a lot of black people going to football, and mid-'70s there was a lot more overt racism around,' he remembers. 'But I didn't feel that at Tottenham. In fact, I always got the impression that there were probably more black fans at Tottenham than was average for the time.

'One of my earliest memories is an away game at Aston Villa. I think we lost 3–2. I was about 14, 15, and I remember seeing a group of black Tottenham fans at Oldham, and that really, really stuck with me. I felt comfortable and I've always felt comfortable at Tottenham – always. Only once in all my time going to Tottenham has there ever been anything whereby I felt a bit ashamed and annoyed at Tottenham fans.

'I was probably in my 20s, and I can't remember the game, but I remember there was a group of guys who were clearly racist and they were making a racist chant, and I remember looking up and feeling absolutely sick.'

Things were changing on the pitch as well as off it in the 1970s, a period when Spurs were gaining a bit of a reputation as a cosmopolitan club. 'That definitely had an effect on me, most definitely,' says Tunde. 'I remember watching the World Cup in Argentina and salivating over this little geezer that Argentina had. I was 15 at the time, and I thought he was the best player in the whole World Cup. Everybody was talking about Leopoldo Luque and Mario Kempes, but this little geezer was the one I liked, Ardiles.

'I was on holiday in Nigeria at the time, watching. The day I got back, Spurs had signed him – the best player in the World Cup, and Tottenham signed him!'

Today, it's difficult to comprehend just what an incredible piece of news this signing was now that the Premiership is packed with foreign players. But back in 1979, securing the services of Osvaldo Ardiles and Ricardo Villa was a quite astonishing feat.

'Bringing an Argentinian over was quite a thing at the time,' remembers Tunde, 'and the fact that there were black players too was important to me as a black kid. There weren't many black people in football, or black football fans, so it was important to me that I supported a club who embraced diversity. Other clubs didn't seem to want to know about black players, but it wasn't a problem at Tottenham, and I love the club for that, I really, really do.'

There's been much debate about the importance of role models and the need for communities to see themselves reflected in the clubs they support. Tunde's experience demonstrates the real benefits of something still often questioned as a piece of political ephemera. His comments on how times have changed again also make interesting reading.

'There's been a period where it's been difficult for me, because Arsenal, their youth teams and schoolboy teams have got a lot of black players, but ours had practically none,' he says. 'Tottenham's my club, always has been, always will be, but that was a problem for me for a while. And seeing Arsenal's first team when they had black Londoners in their side. They had Michael Thomas, who's a Spurs fan, Paul Davis, Rocastle – these were guys I could really identify with, because I come from the same manor. I've looked at Spurs sometimes and been frustrated at why we haven't seemed to make the most of our catchment area. Players like Des Walker, who was once a great player – from Tottenham's doorstep, y'know?

'I had to suffer in silence, but that seems to have changed. Particularly over the past few seasons. We had Campbell, who came up through the ranks, that was good while it lasted, a black Londoner playing for Spurs; Ledley; I'm pleased we got Rohan Ricketts. London is the most cosmopolitan city in the country and it's nice to see that diversity reflected at Spurs.'

As the name of Tottenham's now infamous former captain has come up, what did Tunde think of Spurs fans' reaction to Campbell, especially as one newspaper writer made a high-profile accusation that the vitriol directed at Campbell was fuelled by racism? Tunde simply says he didn't pick up on any racist feeling among the fans he spoke to, but is forthright in his own opinion.

'I would've had no problem with Sol going,' he says, 'but it's the way he did it. He deserves stick 'cos of the way he went about things. What happened cost Tottenham a lot of money. He did what's best for him, and I have no problem with that, but he should have been honest – especially going to Arsenal. It's like he kicked us when we was down. Football being what it is, and us football fans being what we are, he's gonna get stick. And he deserves it.

'Personally, as regards Sol Campbell, I've moved on, and I can't wait till on the pitch we prove to him he's made the wrong decision. Ultimately that's the only way he's really gonna know.'

Being as aware as he is of Tottenham the place as well as the club, what's Tunde's take on the rumours about moving to a new ground?

'I love Tottenham Hotspur to play at Tottenham. I love going to it, I've been going for 30 years. I think it does add something to the London Borough of Haringey being there, but I don't think it's the be-all and end-all for many people. Some of the traders would be affected if Spurs moved, but many people probably couldn't be bothered.

'I think it would be a huge pity if we moved and I don't see there's any reason. As I understand it there's permission to extend the East Stand to make it 44,000; that's a decent enough size. I think we have to do it the right way round. If you get success on the pitch, you'll have a waiting list of people who want to come to the ground, so then you increase capacity. At the moment it just seems cart before the horse.'

Tunde, like most Tottenham fans, has a lot to say about the team's lack of success and the reasons for it, so the obvious question is why does he keep putting himself through it? His answer should be required reading for all those in the game who insist football is 'a business like any other', because what other business's customers would say this?

'Why don't I stop? Because I'm Tottenham, and you know Tottenham's who I am. It's what I am. I'm a season-ticket holder. I've got two season tickets. Each month I go there and see home games. I sometimes go with my wife or one of my children. You know it's poor, it's really poor, and quite often I say to myself I'm not going to renew. But I keep renewing in the hope that this season it will be all right when something changes.

'My eldest son is interested in it, but I must admit it is disappointing because sometimes we go there and the football is quite awful. I bring him, as opposed to my wife, in the hope that he can learn from it. He can learn some good habits. But it's been really, really difficult for him to have a player he can identify with and want to be like.

'It was great when Ginola was there. That was the last time that somebody in a Spurs shirt really excited me. I think my wife felt the same, and my son and even my daughter, who I took occasionally as well. It was somebody who was just that little bit different – somebody with something special and extra.'

But while Tunde has no hesitation in saying the side is 'his', he is circumspect about the chances of fans like him asserting their influence where it matters.

'I don't think the supporters can ever really be involved, because to be involved you've gotta have money,' he says. 'It makes for good copy in the newspapers, the TAG [Tottenham Action Group] or the SOS [Save Our Spurs] stuff, but I don't think it made that much of a difference. The Trust . . . When I first heard about it, I thought it was a good idea, but I think they've effectively been relegated to the part of Enic's PR, like when they endorsed raising season-ticket prices and removal of the cup vouchers. I've no time for the Trust. They made mistakes early on and they've landed themselves with the look of being Enic's puppet.

'It would be good if we could genuinely get a fan's voice on the board, but we need to make sure that fan's voice is genuinely democratic and is not hijacked by people who feel good about the fact that they can rub shoulders with bigwigs.'

It's been a wide-ranging discussion, and now all that remains is to ask some more simple, football questions. For example, what was Tunde's high point as a Spurs fan?

'My high point would have to be 1991, the Cup final,' he says. 'I was right there behind the goal, me and my mate, another black Spurs fan, close to my birthday, it was absolutely it, definitely my highest moment.'

We began by talking about fans' expectations, so what are his – realistically?

'In the next five or ten years, definitely winning the Championship,' he says, without hesitation. 'I think unless that's what the board wants and that's what any manager we get in wants, we'll be in for more midtable mediocrity. We have to want to be the very best, that has to be our ambition. It's absolute rubbish to say it's all down to ground capacity and money.

'We've seen over the last few years that some sides have come from nowhere to challenge, if you consider what Martin O'Neill achieved at Leicester and even Curbishley [at Charlton] is achieving now. We have 36,000 fans week in week out, paying serious money. We even now are only a couple of midfield players and a fit Freddie Kanouté away from having a very decent side. If we can get a manager who can instil in the players the passion and the aggression, and a couple of modern midfielders, there's no reason we can't achieve.'

6

You are my Tottenham: Eleanor Levy

You are my Tottenham
My only Tottenham
You make me happy
When skies are grey
You'll never know just
How much I love you
Until you've taken my Tottenham away

Spurs put the derby blues behind them by beating a lacklustre Aston Villa 2–1 at home, before stumbling again with a depressing 1–0 away defeat at Blackburn. But after a much-needed 3–1 victory against Manchester City, hopes were raised for progress in the League with improved performances. The 5–2 thrashing of Wolves, featuring a Robbie Keane hat-trick and a fantastic goal from on-loan Stephane Dalmat, hinted at an upturn in fortunes, but the scoreline masked what had been a difficult game against the division's whipping boys. A more accurate reflection of the quality of Tottenham's overall play came in their next five matches, all of them lost.

The dreadful run started with Tottenham's annual thrashing in the north-east, 4–0 at Newcastle, the fourth goal culminating in a very public row as Dean Richards berated Kasey Keller for the American goalkeeper's failure to gather a cross. If observers wanted visible proof that there was something seriously wrong in the heart of the club, this was surely it.

The League Cup has been something of a saviour for Tottenham in recent seasons, offering the most realistic avenue for European qualification. So the arrival of Middlesbrough for a midweek quarter-final was seen as an opportunity to lay the ghost of Newcastle to rest. With the scores level at 1–1 after a tight match, however, Spurs lost 5–4 on penalties – though in a sublimely Kafkaesque moment, the official club website insisted the game was a draw.

If these were strange and testing times for regulars at White Hart Lane, how did it all look from a distance? While it's those who attend the games whose voices are heard most, or those who feel involved enough to phone the weekly radio shows which fuel endless football 'debates', the constituency of Spurs supporters encompasses many people who feel more removed. Although the image of the lifelong obsessive is an easy one for the marketing and media executives to hang their latest promotion upon, the truth is that the intensity of most fans' support ebbs and flows along with the rest of their lives.

There would have been a time when Eleanor Levy was one of those who depended on her regular fix of live football at White Hart Lane, when a Tottenham season ticket would have been one of the first things to be rescued in a house fire and when football was a major part of her working life as well as her leisure time. But times change. Now 40, Eleanor is mother of two children, aged six and ten, and is deputy editor on a mass-market women's weekly magazine. For a while, other priorities took over. 'I gave my season ticket up when I had Charlie six years ago,' says Eleanor. 'I'd been since then, but I hadn't been at all for three years. This year I got back into it, mainly because of the kids.'

For Eleanor, it didn't take long for old loyalties to kick in. 'My youngest one, Charlie, suddenly got really into football. Joe, who's ten, isn't that into football, but he suddenly started supporting Arsenal, because all his friends did – and obviously you would, wouldn't you [laughs], if you're not being forced to support anyone else? – and I really didn't want that to happen. As Charlie started getting interested I really wanted to take him to Spurs, then Joe said he wanted to come along as well, so I ended up taking them.

'I've only been a couple of times this year because I couldn't believe how expensive it was. We're going to get membership for next season because they want to start going. And so do I.'

If ever there was proof that, once bitten, the dedicated fan never loses the bug, Eleanor provides it. She moves smoothly into more animated mode as she recounts her reconnection with watching her team live. 'I *knew*, once I started again, that I would get back into it. Because you forget, when you're just seeing them on the television and they're crap, you forget that actually that's only half of it, it's the whole experience of being there is the reason why you go. The whole experience of being a supporter is 'cos you feel part of it, you actually believe you're part of the building and the structure, even though it's completely changed since I first started going. As soon as I went again I knew I wanted to keep going. If I could afford season tickets for the three of us, then I would, but I can't. We are gonna go more regularly from now on, though. And having Charlie be so enthusiastic reminded me of how I used to be when I used to go.'

Eleanor's kids have added an extra dimension to her enjoyment of matchdays, but was she worried about taking them to an environment which can sometimes be aggressive and threatening?

'Not really, although that's one of the reasons why I got seats downstairs in the West Stand, so we could get away easily if we needed to. I didn't really worry. They're used to swearing – they know that words you sometimes use when you're watching football aren't for use in everyday conversation.

'Joe's more of a statto type – he likes the World Cup wallcharts and the strips – so he just sat there and didn't say a word, except occasionally, but afterwards he said he really enjoyed it.

'But Charlie was just going mad, really excited and jumping up and down and knowing all the team, which was great. We were in the first row, so when players came up to take throw-ins, he was just so excited. It was great watching him.'

So much, and yet so little, had happened in the three years since Eleanor had been at White Hart Lane. Indeed, she says she was struck by 'how little it had changed. But I was sitting in the West Stand, where I'd never sat before. I'd always been in the Members' Stand or before that in the Paxton.'

There was one familiar element she did immediately pick up though. 'Spurs fans just haven't changed. The game we went to was the Bolton game, where we lost, and as soon as it started going against us that whole despondency and frustration, the kind of spoilt kid stamping their feet and not getting behind the team, that was the same as I'd always remembered.' It's that controversial point again the fickle nature of the Spurs crowd. Eleanor's aware that it's a view frowned on by many Spurs fans, but she's not afraid to argue her point.

'Andy, my husband, is a Portsmouth fan and I used to go to Fratton Park with him. Seeing how they support their team, even when things aren't going well for them . . . I don't think we're fickle, people are much better than me in that they continue going year in year out without breaks, and they pay an awful lot of money to do it. But the problem is we are very quick to turn on the team when anything goes wrong. I suspect it's because so many people have been going for so long that you just automatically get that feeling of "Oh, God, here we go again."

'But when things go right, I think we're brilliant. I have to say that when I took the kids to the Bolton game I didn't think we were as bad as we'd been in the past. They outplayed us and it was more a kind of glum silence than getting on the back of the team, but I think that's actually worse. One of the criticisms is that people go there, pay their money and say, "Come on, then, entertain me, you're Tottenham", so people have unreal expectations because that Tottenham hasn't existed for years, for probably half the crowd's lifetime.'

Spurs has been a passion for well over half Eleanor's lifetime, so what first attracted her?

'My dad was from Tottenham and was a Tottenham fan. I suppose because he only had girls, me and my sister, he used to take my sister when I was young. I always said I wanted to go and he always said he'd take me when I was older. We were always allowed to stay up and watch *Match of the Day*, and I remember the 1970 World Cup really vividly. It's the first thing I can remember in colour. I was born before '66, but I only remember 'cos I had a World Cup Willy pencil. I don't remember England winning.

'I always felt excluded 'cos my sister Gill could go; she's four years older than me. Then at the age when Dad could've started taking me, it was when all the violence was occurring and he wouldn't. He wouldn't take my sister either. He used to go on his own, and I can still picture him going off to get the 144 bus up to The Angel at Edmonton and leaving us there – we were desperate to go with him.

'Feeling hard done by actually fuelled my interest. I suppose like most dads at the time we didn't spend an awful lot of time with him, but he would sit and talk to us about football. The first match I remember watching was the 1970 FA Cup replay, Chelsea–Leeds. I remember wanting Chelsea to win because I thought Leeds were ugly. I remember I thought Paul Reaney was the most ugly man I'd ever seen in my life. Even at seven, I could see Chelsea were kind of glamorous and rock 'n' roll. That's the first match I remember watching live on the telly.'

It was some time before Eleanor managed to get to see her team in the flesh and, perhaps a foretaste of things to come, times weren't good for them. 'I first went to Spurs the season we went down, so I was 14. Dad took me. We had seats way back in the East Stand. I remember John Lacey was playing and every time he had the ball he'd kick it high up and we'd lose the ball for about five seconds because it would take ages to come down. It was 0–0 against Southampton.'

It doesn't sound an auspicious start, but there's more to football than just results and big but limited defenders, and Eleanor was almost instantly hooked on the atmosphere she encountered, an atmosphere which gave many teenagers of her generation a world that they could get to grips with far removed from home and parents. 'I have to say what I liked about it was the aggression and the threat and the fact that it was such a different life to anything else,' she remembers. 'I started going with my friends, Tottenham fans from school. I was living in Walthamstow at the time.

'It's funny, but my dad stopped going almost as soon as I started. I really got into it and I thought it was really exciting. Then my sister started going out with a guy who used to go, so I started going with them. He was really quiet, but his mate was one of the loudmouths on the Shelf and that was just really exciting because, it was obviously before the seats, but being very young and very short I would be there in the middle of all these shouting and screaming men, and I just thought it was the most exciting thing in the world – even when we were losing 5–0 to Arsenal!'

It's a myth, although one that seems to stick, that women only started going to football after Gazza cried at Italia '90. But, even so, it was unusual to see groups of girls going to the match in the late 1970s and early 1980s. 'I went with friends,' says Eleanor. 'There were usually two, sometimes three, of us. There was usually me and my friend Deborah, and there were another group of girls who also went to Tottenham, but we didn't go together, they went somewhere else. They also used to go and hang out at training and try and talk to the players, but we never really wanted to do that, we just wanted to see the game.

'I didn't go to away games. I went to away games in London, but only places like Craven Cottage. I didn't travel, that wasn't part of my football culture. That was White Hart Lane and feeling part of the White Hart Lane crowd.'

Eleanor doesn't attempt to paint a picture of past perfection lost, but she's honest in her account of what grabbed her affections in formative years, which seem a whole lifetime, not just a couple of decades, ago.

'The crowd seemed louder then. And, this was before the seats, I used to spend whole games standing up and not seeing anything. In Ossie Ardiles's testimonial I was on the Shelf, and I didn't see a ball – only when it went up in the air. I couldn't see anything 'cos there was so many people, but I thought it was one of the most exciting things in the world. It was frustrating: Maradona was playing and it would have been nice to see what he was up to. I much preferred it when I could actually see the game, obviously. But I did like going on the Shelf, and I felt safe there, because I would get scared of any aggression. I remember getting chased by Arsenal fans after a night game and being absolutely terrified; not that they would've done anything. I think, being a girl, I was a lot safer than if I'd been a 15-year-old boy. I remember hearing John Peel being interviewed one time and he said he didn't go to football to get beaten up, but the fact that it was a possibility was part of the whole experience.

'The only thing I can think of in my girlhood that compares was when we went to the airport when the Bay City Rollers were going off to Japan. I wasn't even a Bay City Rollers fan, but my friends were. We got on the Tube and we went to Heathrow, and it took us something like four hours to get there. When we arrived, there were 50 or 60 Rollers fans and they were basically marauding through the terminals trying to find the Bay City Rollers. They were really mouthy and really aggressive, and suddenly the cry went up that Woody or someone had been spotted and everyone just ran. There were 50 teenaged girls just running through the terminal knocking people aside – it was just complete hysteria. We ended up on top of one of the car parks shouting and screaming – and I *never* liked the Rollers, yet I was shouting and screaming and joining in as well! You just get completely caught up in it – it's quite scary really, that pack mentality, but it's something that I did like about football. I'm not sure, would I like it now? I dunno. It was one of those things, though. As I got older as well, I really found it was good stress relief, to let your aggression out; there is nothing quite like shouting and screaming at referees and that sort of thing.'

What has changed for the better is the absence of a particular sort of aggression. 'When I was younger, as a woman going to football matches there was often quite a lot of sexual threat if I was on my own. I remember once being followed down the High Road by someone who was, erm, basically offering to cum over my arse, all the way down Tottenham High Road. That kind of thing used to happen a lot. Obviously I'm older now so that's probably got something to do with it, and if I'm with kids, that will too. It did used to be quite a dangerous place to go, not just for the violence; it was threatening and you just don't get that sense any more. I think a lot of that is because there's more women going, and maybe the fact it's become more corporate, and it's so expensive – people find other ways to get their thrills and they don't have to spend so much money doing it.'

As she grew up, the pull of Spurs began to compete with other things – particularly music. 'I did get quite into music and, especially when I was young, I tended to be quite obsessive about things. There just wasn't space to be obsessive about two things. I did still go – I remember going down to the Dell to see us play Southampton when I was at college, but it wasn't a regular thing.

'I stayed in London to go to college. I knew I wanted to be a journalist and the two courses I applied for happened to be in London. For the first year I was at college I kept going.'

Soon taken on by *Record Mirror*, Eleanor's drift from the terraces at Spurs continued as she embraced the life of the music journalist. But the lure of the Lilywhites soon asserted itself again and a combination of circumstances led her back. 'It was a dream job going out all the time to gigs and things,' she says. 'Music had been my big hobby and it suddenly became my job, and I think I needed to go back to something that wasn't related to my job, where I wouldn't be talking about work or bumping into press officers. In the end, one of the people I went to Spurs with was a press officer for Phonogram – but it was just a release, really. And then I managed to find "like-minded people".'

A new regular crew was soon established. 'When I was in my 20s and working at *Record Mirror*, we used to go with some people after work. We'd get the Tube and meet at Seven Sisters, Mike Gardner, Adrian Thrills and another guy called Paul Marcus, who was a theatre director and had been a Spurs fan for years, and occasionally there'd be other people there as well. We'd all meet at Seven Sisters and walk up the High Road, go to McDonald's; always get the same thing; then walk up to the ground; always go in the same entrance; walk through the Paxton Road end; always stop off to get a Sports Quart – before they banned alcohol you used to get these huge plastic things of beer – and then go round to the bottom of the Shelf and always stand in exactly the same place. There was a guy there who always used to burp and it never felt quite right until you heard him burping – we used to call him The Bullfrog.

'The height of that was 1985, probably the only year in my life when we actually stood a chance of winning the title, and you had to do it, and you had to wear the same clothes, because we were such a good team then and it all seemed to click and if you did anything wrong you just knew that would be it.'

Work contacts soon opened a route into football journalism, not through the traditional channels – Julie Welch was the only female sports reporter on the less-than-enlightened sports desks at the nationals at the time – but through the fanzines that were then proliferating.

'When I was at *Record Mirror*, I met Stuart Mutler through someone I was working with, Iestyn George,' remembers Eleanor. 'Stuart had just started *The Spur* fanzine and asked me if I wanted to write for it, so I wrote about Graham Roberts, who was my hero, still is.

'I did it just because I wanted to, and then I lost my job when they shut *Record Mirror*. So I was looking around for a job and I saw an advert for *90 Minutes*. Paul Hawksbee and Dan Goldstein had started it in Dan's bedroom in Blackheath and Dennis Publishing had bought it. They'd just started turning it from a serious magazine into a kind of satirical and funny and serious proper fans' magazine, basically, and it was completely staffed by real fans. It was such a laugh to work there.

'They were paying really bad wages, but I didn't care – I'd got a really nice payoff and I just wanted a job because I'd never been out of work. The idea of writing about football and actually working within that area was fantastic. It turned out that they were all big music fans and they were impressed by the fact that I worked for a music magazine, and I think that's why I got the job. Everyone was quite young, and nobody even mentioned the fact that I was female; it was never an issue, and it was just great.'

Football journalism has always been a bastion of traditionalism, but as Eleanor started at *90 Minutes* a new generation shaped by a different set of values were beginning to assert themselves – many of whom had cut their teeth in the club fanzines. Oddly enough, the criticism Eleanor most remembers came from someone else who had made their name on the alternative scene, and who, at the time, wrote for the well-regarded West Ham fanzine *Fortune's Always Hiding* (*FAH*). 'I remember *The Spur* getting slagged off by Phill Jupitus, who was involved with *Fortune's Always Hiding*. I'd interviewed Billy Bragg and Phill had been around but I hadn't had the chance to talk to him, and I read an interview where he slagged *The Spur* off for being staffed by professional journalists! It really pissed me off!' No wonder, for *FAH* was produced by a professional photographer, some regular contributors to *Time Out* and the music press, and media bloke Phill Jupitus himself. 'I would have thought he more than anyone would have known that we might've been journalists, but we were writing about something we loved,' says Eleanor.

As for the mainstream press, Eleanor remembers that the old guard 'really didn't like the new breed who were coming through', but she doesn't reckon this was to do with being a woman in a profession dominated by men. 'When I became editor at *90 Minutes*, I had to do all these radio interviews about being a woman in a man's world, which were incredibly tedious,' she says. 'They always said, "Don't they treat you differently because you're a woman?" And they did, but they'd treat all the other people on *90 Minutes* differently, too; it was a generational thing, it was an outlook thing. We didn't wear bad suits, we didn't have huge collections of pornography back in our bachelor flats. We had a life, basically, and football was part of our lives; we just had a different attitude towards it.'

In fact, Eleanor always retained her fan's perspective. 'I hated going in the press box at Tottenham,' she says. 'I only ever did it once, and I really hated the fact that everyone sat there being so cynical and you couldn't shout and scream. I had my season ticket, so I used to go with the fans.'

Football journalism at that time was also operating in a more innocent environment. 'Halcyon days,' remembers Eleanor. 'You could ring up grounds and training grounds and get to talk to people on the phone, and we spoke to loads of players without having to have agents or go through press officers or, more importantly, without having to go through the people who were paying lots of money to sponsor them. That was the thing that was really frustrating, and at the end why I was glad to get out of it.'

Neither was Eleanor hung up on meeting the stars she'd watched on the pitch. 'There were always players I really liked, but I never really wanted to meet them,' she says. 'When I was at *Record Mirror,* Hoddle and Waddle brought out "Diamond Lights" and I met them. There was a big piss-up to launch the record and I went along and got horribly drunk and was probably falling over myself saying, "Hi, you're fantastic", then I had to go and interview them and that made me realise that footballers aren't that interesting. That wasn't the reason I wanted to do it. I just liked the fact I was finding out what was happening in football. Talking to managers I used to find interesting.'

By the time *90 Minutes* closed in 1997, Eleanor was already a mum to three-year-old Joe and, with the imminent arrival of Charlie, everything was changing. Visits to White Hart Lane were no longer quite so important and, she remembers, the truth was it was not that hard to stop. 'It was partly because Tottenham were so awful,' she says. 'It coincided with George Graham really, and I deeply resented him being manager.

'When I first started going, it was just after Terry Neill wrecked the club and it always seemed to me that when George came it was so totally wrong, not just to have a former Arsenal manager but *that* former Arsenal manager managing the team. Just him, as a person, it was so obvious he should never have been anywhere near White Hart Lane. Even if he'd won the FA Cup three times in a row, it would've been wrong. It just wasn't supposed to happen, so that contributed to it. It didn't make me make the effort when I had two kids under four. If we hadn't had George Graham in charge, I suspect I wouldn't have had a complete break, but then once I got out of the habit it was just a question of getting back into it again.'

This time it felt like a more complete break than when one

teenage obsession replaced another. Nevertheless, Spurs were never far away, and strangely enough it was one of the club's endless series of crises that she says 'really got me back into it'. This was to be the controversial departure of Sol Campbell to Arsenal.

'When Charlie was born, Andy had interviewed Sol Campbell so he'd got Sol to write a "welcome to the world"-type autograph that we were going to give to Charlie when he was older, and he'd autographed this big poster for Joe. So I was just absolutely devastated because now I'd say to Charlie, "You've got this", and he's a kind of Gooner turncoat bastard. I just thought it was so wrong that he'd done that and so wrong that that had been allowed and that got me so angry that I suddenly felt like Tottenham needed me again. It sounds stupid, but it got my interest going again.'

During Eleanor's time on *Record Mirror*, agit-popsters The Redskins released a single which urged listeners to 'take no heroes, only inspiration'. Did the Campbell affair mean this is a message she passes on to her kids?

'No, you've always got to have players as heroes, especially when you're younger,' she says. 'I don't think you can have the concept of the club; you need to relate it to individuals.'

But she does have a down-to-earth take on the importance invested in footballers as role models. 'They're obviously not worthy, of course they're not worthy. I get really cross when people are seen to be role models. They're young, not particularly well-educated blokes, who are obviously going to get into trouble off the pitch, just like people do in the normal world. It's a world where they're cosseted and looked after by people and then let off the leash, with a lot of money.'

Far from worrying about the example that footballers set, she says, her kids 'don't care, they don't read tabloid newspapers, and that's where most of it is. Unless it's on *Goals on Sunday*, or *The Premiership*, then Charlie, the six-year-old, certainly wouldn't know about it, and Joe wouldn't care anyway. Me and Andy have always been into music – Joe's Joe because of Joe Strummer – so he knows all about punk and stuff. Things that footballers do are nothing compared to Sid Vicious stabbing his girlfriend in a hotel room, which he knows all about.'

Eleanor's also able to give an insight into the way that kids approach football now. 'Charlie is really into that *Fifa 2004* game, and, to him, that is almost as real as real-life football. Part of the reason why he wanted Freddie Kanouté on the back of his shirt, even though at that point he hadn't seen him play, was because he scored loads of goals in *Fifa 2004*. It's interesting watching him. He's only interested in what's happening on the pitch and the players' names and who they play for.'

So much for her son's favourite, but what about Eleanor's own favourite player and Spurs side?

'The '85 team,' she says after some thought, 'because of Roberts, because we had, I guess, beauty and brawn, and they just seemed like a real team rather than lots of stars brought together.

'Roberts was the ultimate Tottenham player; we've never replaced him, he was totally my hero even though I know, particularly when he was at Rangers, I wouldn't get on with him personally. He was a dirty bastard, but he could play. He was hard but fair. Adrian Thrills, who I used to go to games with, I think he used to share a flat with Pat Nevin and I remember him saying that Pat Nevin had played against Graham Roberts and Roberts had kicked him up in the air a few times, but Pat Nevin said he was "hard but fair" and I always thought that, from a fellow pro, that was a good comment. He just never stopped trying. You'd think he was just a complete bruiser, and then he'd do an absolutely inch-perfect 30-yard pass or a screaming goal. He could actually stop the other team playing, which, over the years, most Spurs teams can't.'

For her most disappointing experience, Eleanor cites 'the break-up of that Venables side, when we had Ruddock, and Erik [Thorstvedt] in goal and Nayim, so you had three characters who the crowd really got behind. It was the only time when the Tottenham crowd really were different, because you had so many players in that side who the crowd idolised, so you really enjoyed being part of the crowd and the whole team responded.

'I remember being in the office and Paul Hawksbee saying, "Right, we've just found out Des Walker's coming and Andy Townsend's coming, they're definitely coming to Tottenham," in that close season and then it all just fell apart. And that was just so disappointing. I suppose that was the beginning of me losing my blind optimism that I always used to have.'

However, the public dispute between Terry Venables and chairman Alan Sugar didn't prompt Eleanor to get involved in the vociferous fans' campaigns of the time. 'I try and avoid things like that,' she says. 'I hate meetings, mainly because when I was younger I used to go to quite a few political meetings and I don't like getting involved in that kind of thing. I think people do because they feel that they want to have a say, they want to feel empowered, and that always makes me feel incredibly depressed because it makes you realise how little power you actually have – which I know is a very defeatist attitude.

'I think it's really good for fans to get involved and it's even better if clubs actually listen to them, but ultimately I guess I don't care enough any more.'

She does care passionately about the changing relationship with local rivals Arsenal, though, offering a very honest appraisal of where things are. 'The moment that changed me as a Tottenham fan was when Arsène Wenger took over at Arsenal. The one thing we had over them was that for all the Chippy Bradys and Anders Limpars occasionally playing there and being flash, they were boring and they churned out results and they were a team, but nobody would really get any joy out of watching them. I was watching them on Sky, and Wenger took Ray Parlour off and brought Vieira on, and within seconds Vieira did this fantastic Hoddlesque pass. I just remember watching it and thinking: "Shit – he should be a Tottenham player, and Wenger should be Tottenham manager." I still think it's a mistake: that he shouldn't be at Arsenal.

'I was talking to an Arsenal fan recently and he said: "We don't really care about you, you're not in our league", and I couldn't really argue. And I believe he really thinks that. They don't need to beat us to prove anything, whereas my greatest moment as a Tottenham fan was when we beat them in the semi-final at Wembley. That's probably the most excitement I've ever had in my life. It was typical Tottenham because not only did we beat them, it's how we beat them. It was the last moment when we really had that moral superiority – we were beautiful and successful, and they were dull and crap. It's probably the worst thing that's ever happened because it's never been the same again.'

While she is measured in her assessment of where the local rivals stand in relation to each other, Eleanor admits she's not above succumbing to a gut dislike of the old enemy.

'I do still absolutely loathe Arsenal and everything about them,' she says. 'I remember coming back from the semi-final in '93 when we lost and I'd had, erm, a few drinks to make myself feel better and I was walking home. There was a park opposite the flat where I was living and there were a couple of eight- and nine-year-old boys. One of them was wearing an Arsenal shirt and I was wearing my Tottenham shirt, and he started laughing at me. So I turned round and told him to fuck off [laughs]. The fact that I was an educated, professional woman in my twenties telling an eight-year-old kid to fuck off because he dissed my football team . . . I still really loathe them and the sooner Wenger goes the better, really, because I can go back to hating them.'

Eleanor is also blunt about what she expects for the club. 'I did once say that I didn't want to die until they'd won the title, but at this stage I'm going to be living for hundreds of years because I can't see that happening,' she says ruefully. 'I suppose what I'd really like is to watch the team and feel proud to be a Tottenham fan again.'

7

It's up to you, you Lilywhites: Jim Duggan

The cockerel crows, the whistle blows
And now we're in the game
It's up to you, you Lilywhites
To live up to your name
There's other teams from other towns and some are great or small
But the famous Tottenham Hotspur are the greatest of them all

For many years, Tottenham Hotspur v. Manchester United was the glamour fixture in the English football calendar, stemming back to a series of epic encounters in the 1960s. In December 2003, it was just another game, especially for United, who viewed it as simply another opportunity to glean vital away points in their quest for the title. More damning from Tottenham's point of view was the hope of most of the club's fans merely to avoid an embarrassing thrashing.

First-half goals from John O'Shea and Ruud van Nistelrooy, again as a result of poor defending, sealed the result, with a brief second-half rally and a scrambled goal from Gus Poyet at least saving any home blushes. Defeat to the champions was no disgrace, but yet another loss in the next League game, this time to Portsmouth, was, as Spurs succumbed to two Patrik Berger goals with barely a whisper of defiance.

A month of misery was rounded off with the fifth home League defeat of the season, this time to Charlton. Spurs did not actually play that badly, but the symbolism of the result was obvious: a well-organised side assembled for a fraction of the cost that it took to build the Tottenham team had come to the Lane and showed Spurs how to win football matches. That it was engineered by Scott Parker

– the best midfielder Glenn Hoddle never had – and Addicks boss Alan Curbishley, long-rumoured to be Hoddle's replacement, only added to the irony.

During the month of December, Spurs had played seven League and Cup games, winning just two and losing the rest. It meant that the class of 2003 had the unenviable distinction of recording Tottenham's worst League position at the turn of the year since 1910. Worse still, in a 'league table' for the year Spurs would have finished firmly at the bottom. This was the definition of relegation form.

Events away from the games provided no respite. Pressed from all sides to be decisive in their appointment of a successor to Hoddle, the directors chose instead to hold what they had. After speculation linking everyone to the job from Martin O'Neill to Harry Redknapp, David Pleat and Chris Hughton were given the go-ahead to manage and coach the first team until 'the right man' could be brought in, probably at the end of the season.

The logic of taking time to make the appointment, cited by chairman Daniel Levy as the most important decision the club had faced for years, was sound – why rush into bringing in a new head coach just to keep impatient fans happy? This, it was reasoned, was what had happened in the past. Unfortunately for Levy, healthy scepticism runs deep at White Hart Lane, with many arguing that the reason for the delay was simply that the club did not have a clue who they wanted to bring in, whether they could get him and (if he did arrive) what kind of management structure would be in place.

Even when Spurs announced what they imagined to be good news, it backfired and only increased the suspicions of those who felt Levy and Enic did not have Tottenham's best interests at heart. Just ahead of the club's AGM, Spurs went public on a new share issue that would, the sales blurb promised, raise £15 million for a greatly strengthened transfer fund.

A sizeable number of Spurs fans are well versed in all matters financial and not just because, as season-ticket holders, they are used to having to deal with large sums of money. The ranks of accountants, City traders and corporate managers who support the club soon put word around that there was more to the share deal than met the eye.

The details were a familiar blend of PLC-speak and financial find-the-lady – now you see the money, now you don't. Suffice to say

Loyal supporters: fans in full voice away at Old Trafford.

Hope springs: Jamie Redknapp leads Spurs out at Birmingham
for the opening game of the season. (© Offside)

Not long now Glenn: the King of White Hart Lane,
just before his early-season sacking. (© Offside)

Bruce Lee: 'Maybe some kids
go to Cannes and Hollywood; I
got to go to Burnley and
Norwich.' (© Derek Ridgers)

Catherine Saunders: 'I always
have the fixture list by my
phone. So if anyone wants me
to go out somewhere, I check
that first.' (© Derek Ridgers)

You need hands: coach Chris Hughton and Acting Manager David Pleat share their relief at the last-gasp win at Leicester. (© Offside)

Aubrey Morris holds a picture of himself and England captain Bobby Moore. 'I organised the first air travel for football supporters.' (© Derek Ridgers)

We all dream . . .

. . . of a team . . .

. . . of Robbie Keanes.

The player of the season gives another display
of his trademark goal celebration. (all © Offside)

Junior Spurs fans Ella and Isaac
Davies Oliveck play their part in
funding the squad's wages.

Danny Spalding and Alfie: 'I've
always tried to tell him about the
importance of staying loyal.'
(© Derek Ridgers)

Norman Jay: 'We were all soul
boys. We went to Sheffield,
Stoke, Wigan, all of these cities
had clubs. Saturday was like
killing two birds with one stone.'
(© Derek Ridgers)

Fallen star: Freddie Kanouté started with a bang, then faded after a controversial trip to the African Nations Cup. (© Offside)

Stand up if you hate Arsenal: Spurs fans in vociferous mood at White Hart Lane for the climactic game against their hated rivals. (© Offside)

Lee Benjamin: 'Can you imagine no Spurs? It's unthinkable.' (© Derek Ridgers)

that under the terms of the issue, 'convertible redeemable preference shares' could be bought for a discount on the current price of ordinary shares but could then be switched in three years' time to ordinary share status – in other words an investor could buy shares on the cheap. Enic would underwrite the scheme and, with predictions that most shareholders would waive their options to take up the offer, would therefore significantly increase their stake without having to pay a premium. They could also request other shareholders to waive the rule on making an offer for the entire stock of the company, once Enic's stock exceeded 30 per cent of the total.

The scheme had already reportedly led to resignations: non-executive director Howard Shore and finance director Paul Viner had both left, claiming, apparently, that the share issue was unnecessary and would dilute the influence of smaller shareholders (though there was the inevitable suspicion that they were aggrieved Enic would not be forced to make an offer on their existing shares). Others, while pleased money was being raised without incurring debt, smelt a profiteering rat, an accusation Levy predictably denied. Coupled with suspicions that Levy's move to claim greater control was also designed to head off a proposed scheme set up by the Supporters' Trust to buy and pool the shares held by fans and thus gain some influence at PLC level, and with whiffs of a takeover later in the year beginning to waft around the City, it was entirely understandable that an air of mistrust was growing.

One of the best sources of well-informed gossip and comment on Spurs is the 'TopSpurs' website, run by Jim Duggan, a 35-year-old transport consultant, and it's a regular port of call for fans looking for something to anchor themselves to when the internal politics at the club get stormy. The site's roots lay in Jim's move away from London to college in Leeds between 1987 and 1991, breaking a regular period of support stretching back to 1977. When he returned to London and started going to Spurs matches again, he soon began to look around for other supporters to contact.

'A bloke introduced me to various people, including Bruce Lewis who ran that site "The Legend" and ran a mailing list called the Spurs List,' recalls Jim. 'There were a lot of e-mails going around and it seemed quite informed, quite a lot of interesting people on it. And after a while, I thought, "I'll have a go at this." What I wanted to do was get all the Spurs results on a website and that would be my contribution. So I developed this massive spreadsheet and I was halfway through doing that and I thought, I'm going to go back on and start this website.

'That was 5 September 2000. We beat Everton 3–2 at home. Rebrov's first goals were in that game. I think it took about four to six months to get all the results up. And I started getting attendances and goal-scorers and a few other bits; it's sort of grown from that.'

'TopSpurs' has become far more than just a record of Spurs games, with Jim's editorial now a major draw.

'I just put a few comments before the game and a few after the game; it ended up being the editorial. In effect, you're sort of talking to yourself, which is a bit weird. But after a while I noticed a few people signing the guest book, so I just wondered how these people found it. I went up to a game at Man City and bought a football magazine when the train was delayed. Then I noticed, fucking hell, they've got my website as the fans' site. I was just staring at it for ages. I thought, "How did they find that?" That was the first time I really knew that other people were reading it.

'The amount of time I spend on it is variable, that's the advantage of being freelance, although sometimes I'm away for a while. If there's something going on, I might spend about an hour. Doing the match reports used to be the most enjoyable, although after the first season it started to be a bit of a drag with so many dismal performances, so I thought sod it, I'll just put a couple of comments up. It's just like a hobby really. The site's free, come and read it if you want.

'I get about 4,500 hits a day now, that's a weekday. I know quite a lot of people check in when they get into their office, which is flattering and makes me pull my finger out if I can't be bothered to write anything. For every couple of good comments I get, I get one slagging me off. I think, well, don't fucking read it.'

Putting up with flak is something that's inevitable if you decide to run a high-profile website, but it has its positive moments too.

'When the website had been going a few months, I got this message in the guest book,' says Jim. 'It was from Ricky Villa saying, "I'll be over for a couple of games around Christmas time, to see Spurs play Arsenal." There's an e-mail address there and I didn't even bother looking, I thought y'know, people often sign in under their favourite player's name. After a couple of months, a few people asked me, "Is that the real Ricky Villa?", because they'd checked the e-mail address and it was an Argentinian address. I thought, "It can't be, can it?" But I sent an e-mail and it's him! I couldn't believe it. He mailed me back, then at the Fulham League Cup game that we won 2–1, just along the row from me he's sitting about three seats further down. He had a bloke with him to help him out with a bit of English, but I couldn't believe it – Ricky Villa's in my row! And everyone's giving it "There's only one Ricky Villa", then the people in front started looking round. What a great character. He actually got the Tube to the game, then about three minutes before the end he just got up and walked off into the night. Great bloke.'

Many of the fans interviewed for this book became Tottenham supporters by chance, because of a particular game that made an impression on them or because the reputation of the club appealed to them. But Jim's indulging a passion that has been handed down.

'My father was a big supporter of Spurs for most of the '60s. Before that he used to watch all the London teams, but Spurs was his favourite and the Double clinched it. When he had me in 1969, he named me after Jimmy Greaves. I suppose I was destined to become a Spurs fan after that.

'I was born in Hendon, so geographically it was about the nearest club. Maybe QPR was about the same distance, but they don't really count, do they? I lived in Leeds for four years between 1987 and 1991, which means I missed the big game in '91 – well, both big games in '91 – but that's the way it goes, isn't it?'

Watching Spurs remained a family affair for some time. 'I used to go with my dad from 1977 up to 1987,' Jim remembers. 'I used to prefer to go with my mates, but it's just the sort of thing you did with your family really. My mum used to go to four or five games a year. She used to go with my dad in the '60s and she used to do the queuing up at five in the morning to get European tickets and stuff like that. My dad worked as a milkman then, so before his round he would drop her off, do his round and then come and pick her up.'

Jim's parents rarely go to games now, but Jim acknowledges his dad is a character many Spurs fans would recognise. 'Dad still goes every now and then. He's been moaning about Spurs since I was a little nipper – "There's always something wrong down there" – the same old record. He always used to say it was quite expensive: "Where's all the money going? They must be raking it in." The comment as a kid I still remember now is, "We haven't had a good centre-half since Mike England"; it's all stuff like that.'

Jim's dedication to the cause was fuelled by his early experiences of following Spurs away from home, again with his father.

'I started going to away games in 1978, the Notts County 3–3 game, where we were losing 3–1. Johnny Pratt will always be a personal Spurs hero, as he rescued Spurs in that one. He got two goals, one a 30-yarder I'll never forget. We went to about five that year: Bristol Rovers away and a few London ones. So it was quite enjoyable.

'Spurs didn't really play that different away from home, sometimes they played even better. I suppose there was a fair bit of trouble going on, but I didn't seem to see any of that as a little kid. We often used to be at the home end anyway.'

Jim reflects on how differently fans approached matches in those days, even long trips away. 'It was just like going to a normal game for me,' he says. 'Just turn up on the day and pay on the gate. Now, if a kid's dad took him to see Spurs he'd have to book months in advance.

'It should have been the highlight of the week, but I didn't think like that, it was just something I did. I didn't really perceive myself to be that lucky, but looking back I suppose I was pretty lucky to go to Spurs. But as kids you just get on with it.'

Once he returned from college and started earning, Jim was soon into the swing of following Spurs regularly, owning both a home and away season ticket. But the magic of away trips has waned. 'I jacked the away season ticket in,' he says. 'I've never been convinced that they actually want Spurs supporters to travel away to watch Spurs. To get an away season ticket they charge you £29 a game plus a £35 admin charge per season ticket, so if you've got two season tickets coming to the same address you're charged £70. The admin must be someone stuffing envelopes! And also, the football wasn't that good. There are people who go away from home to watch Spurs no matter how bad they are. But now with the standard of football, I pick and choose.

'The away games were more enjoyable than the home games for a while, just because of the atmosphere that was generated, but it just got so that a great day out was ruined by 90 minutes of football.'

Several generations of players have pulled on the white shirt since Jim's been watching, and his choice of favourite side may come as a surprise.

It's up to you, you Lilywhites

'My favourite side, this is like that bit out of *Ripping Yarns*, I can name the 1977–78 side: Daines, Naylor, Holmes, Hoddle, McAllister, Perryman, Pratt, McNab, Duncan, Lee, Taylor. I suppose I sort of regard them as my favourite team.'

There have undoubtedly been better sides in Spurs' history, but Jim explains that it's his own memories of a vivid season, when Spurs won promotion back to the top flight just one season after the humiliation of relegation, rather than any judgement on the relative quality of the team, that inform his choice.

'That '77–'78 season is one of those seasons, even now, that I can remember with so much detail. The last game of the season, rather than going down to Southampton, I went to watch Spurs reserves. There was a crowd of about 1,000 and I thought that was the best place to get to be part of the Spurs atmosphere without actually being there. I think we won 5–3. Ralph Coates played, and as we were walking out the announcement comes through that the final whistle's blown at the Dell, Spurs have drawn and got promoted. Everyone was jumping up in the air and I cracked me head on the Paxton where there was a slight overhang on the walkway.'

Jim's favourite player is also a surprise from a generation of fans who grew up watching Glenn Hoddle. 'Graham Roberts,' he says without hesitation, 'just ahead of Perryman. It's just I suppose Roberts had that bit of magic about him, but Perryman was my favourite for Spurs for years. He really was Tottenham, he was what Spurs were about, more worthwhile, more noble.

'What happened in the UEFA Cup final in 1984 cemented his place in Spurs' history and as my favourite. We were trailing 1–0 at home and Ossie hit the bar from a yard out. Then, I can still see it now, Roberts was charging through the middle of the Anderlecht box, with defenders seemingly hanging off him as he went. He had the most amazing vision to chest the ball, rather than heading it, to create a certain goal-scoring chance, and I thought that was just the most brilliant thing he could have done. He was also first up to take a penalty, which he scored in the shoot-out. I also seem to remember a vital goal-line clearance against Hajduk Split in the semi when they had taken the ball around Clemence and it needed Robbo flying at full stretch across the goalmouth to clear off the line. While he was in our side, you felt anything could have happened, and players like him are few and far between.'

Jim remembers that cup run with particular pleasure. 'The thing

I really wanted Spurs to do was to win that UEFA Cup in '84,' he says, 'because that was my Spurs team being as good as some of the other ones I'd heard about. I know winning the UEFA Cup is not like winning the Championship, but for me that winning in Europe feeling . . . I thought that was the thing we'd got to do.'

The final of that year's competition was not a classic game of football, but the climax was one of the great moments in Tottenham history, with high drama in a penalty shoot-out in which emotions lurched up and down. Danny Thomas became a legend for missing a penalty and third-choice goalkeeper Tony Parks emerged a hero for saving two.

'I actually regard the 1984 final as my favourite Spurs game. It was just *the* game. I think we were 4–3 up on penalties when Danny Thomas steps up to take one. I found myself getting colder. I thought surely there must be somebody else they could call. The penalty was saved and you go from thinking that penalty could have won the cup to if they scored, they're level again. Five minutes of thinking you're there, then it's gone. But even under all that, all of a sudden you hear this chant of "one Danny Thomas", and it sort of grew and grew; I think you can still hear it on the video now. It was just one of those brilliant moments. I think Roberts went to put his arm round him as well, as he was walking back.

'I also remember from that game, my dad had this routine where we drove down there and we went up Devonshire Hill Road and we parked almost within a metre of the same place every time. We got there this time and all the road was full up, so we go back out on the Great Cambridge and we park just a little bit round the corner. I was so superstitious, I thought, "Oh, Christ, this is it, this is real bad luck." Then that flashed through my head when Danny Thomas missed, that we parked in the wrong place!'

Before the days of Champions League football, which has arguably made many fans over-familiar with matches in Europe, there was an exotic feel to games against foreign opposition. But for Spurs fans, that experience was all part of the package.

'As a kid, it just seemed normal for Spurs to be there, in Europe,' says Jim. 'When we were little kids, like five or six, we should have been out playing on bikes or something, but my dad had his stack of football programmes of the '60s and '70s, and I looked through them and marked my favourites like Union Textiles of Arad and the old

Communist-style stadiums and clubs like Tbilisi, Grasshoppers, all those names. European football seemed so glamorous, the James Bond lifestyle of football. I'd think it would be great to see Spurs out in a place like that, and they'd go out there and win.'

Jim retains a strong sense of the magic he associated with his team, magic that inevitably exercised a powerful influence on a young boy. 'It just seemed that Spurs were the greatest. My dad had fed me all these great facts about Spurs, that they were the first team to win a cup outside of their league, first team to win the Double, and all the great players we had.

'If you look back, there are a few consistent teams like the Evertons and the Liverpools and the other lot that used to win the Championship every now and then, or more regularly than bloody Spurs did, but when you look at the games people remembered, it was like Spurs were always at the forefront of doing things. I just used to think I was lucky enough to be brought up with this great club.

'I took a lot of it for granted. It's only now . . . looking back after the 13 years since we won the Cup in '91 as we've gradually gone to lower and lower levels. What are we now? We're just a normal team. I thought no matter what happens it would always come right, we would always have this sort of magic associated with the club. It was complete childish nonsense in a way, but you always thought that would guide Spurs through.'

While Jim recognises that his view of the game changed as he got older, he's also critical of the real changes in football. 'Every football story you read in the paper now is about money rather than what is actually happening on the pitch,' he says. 'It's about people being transferred rather than the actual nitty-gritty of the game. So I think a lot of the magic stops with money, bit of a cliché I know, but it all seems like businesses competing against each other now. We never used to win the Championship, but we had a place in the world, we were the cup team. Now, the focus has drifted towards the Premiership, grinding out 1–0s away to Middlesbrough or whatever, it's more important than a special cup win somewhere.'

In some respects, Jim's increasing cynicism about the link between the club and its supporters comes from his running of 'TopSpurs'. 'Doing the website, I've found out a lot more about the internal running of the club and the politics and failures,' he says. 'I may be naive but a few years ago I assumed those who worked for Spurs were people who actually wanted to be at Spurs, that they were like Spurs supporters and they wanted to do well there. Then I remember going in the ticket office and there was a letter on the wall saying, "Thank you for your letter of congratulations to Arsenal on winning the Double." From the Goons! I would have not only sacked them, I would have slaughtered them before I would have sacked them! If that was a business and you sent your big competitors a congratulations for winning an order off you . . . well, that wouldn't go down in business, but somehow it's allowed in football.'

After this, it comes as no surprise to hear that Jim wasn't overjoyed when he heard former Arsenal legend George Graham had been appointed manager. Initially, Jim had the same attitude as most Tottenham fans.

'I must admit, when he joined I thought let's give him a go, so I wasn't that anti. I was pissed off that they'd got him, I couldn't realistically see what he was going to do for Spurs, but then somehow or other with Gross's team he won the League Cup, which was great to see Spurs win no matter who was in control. That gave him some breathing space, and then in the summer for Europe he signed Korsten, Perry and Leonhardsen. I could still tolerate him a little bit, but that Kaiserslautern game where he dropped Ginola, that was it. I couldn't believe that he was putting himself in front of the club. Ginola was my favourite Spurs player by miles at the time, I thought he was brilliant, and Graham dropped him and then we let in those two last-minute goals.

'Then you had the Newcastle 6–1 away. Of all the things you accept you had to take with Graham, one thing is that we were not going to get hammered, even though it might be boring. And that was just shocking, so I was really on the anti with him.

'That Kaiserslautern game, that's my biggest-ever Spurs disappointment. I felt numb, I felt sick to the stomach. So yeah, I hated Graham in the end.'

When times are tough, football fans need to get pleasure from the strangest moments, and Jim remembers George Graham's sacking as something almost on a par with winning a trophy.

'I was in Chelmsford for a meeting when he got sacked. My mate who works in the City, an Everton fan, called and said, "Graham's been sacked." It was about a quarter past two in the afternoon and I

said, "If you're winding me up, I'm going to come and kill you."
Then I start getting more calls and it turns out he has gone.

'It wasn't like winning the Cup, but it was like all of a sudden
you've been let out of prison. I went down to the City with my mate
whose boss is a Spurs fan, we were toasting and having a great old
time, and I went home and had a bet on Glenn Hoddle being the
next Spurs manager. With all the drink I put more on than I should
have done, but we got our man and I got about £450.'

Like many, Jim was convinced that Hoddle would turn things
around for Spurs. 'When he arrived at Spurs, I thought, this is going
to be it,' he says. 'But it didn't work out like that. I can't find it in my
heart to slag Hoddle off, you just feel sorry for the geezer. It's just
something around Spurs at the moment, no matter who was there
you think there would be no way Spurs could ever get back to the
sort of level of confidence that they had before, where there were
four teams in the English League and Spurs would be one of the
four. That's all we really want, to win the Cup final every three years,
every three years to be around that sort of area.

'I think it took a long time for the fans to realise that there was
any problem. I can count myself in that. But there's got to be
something better than laughing at Arsenal losing in Europe for us to
look forward to.'

The mood of Tottenham's demoralised supporters at the time was
not helped by the rumours that the board was looking to move away
from White Hart Lane – or even do the unthinkable and share with
Arsenal. The arguments seemed to centre on the potential of the
existing stadium for expansion, and there were conflicting schools of
thought among supporters over the best way forward. Jim puts one
perspective. 'I want Spurs to be in Tottenham. It's important to me.
I could handle somewhere like Picketts Lock; Spurs have moved
three times since we started, after all. But it just seems such a late
'90s idea, that you need to move to a new stadium because your one's
100 years old.

'I've been all round the grounds and Spurs have got the nicest new
stadium. At Old Trafford you've got about half an inch of space when
you sit in your seat, but at Spurs – apart from those bloody pillars that
we could do with getting rid of – we've got a good stadium, good
facilities. When Spurs start doing well, the argument is that the
ground will fill up, but they've got planning permission to build that

East Stand up to 44,000. If they really were concerned about getting fans in the ground, they wouldn't have two tiers of executive boxes. They'd knock them out and get another couple of thousand in.

'It just seems there's so many other important things at the moment – Spurs have got a home, we own it, we can't really sell it on for a massive profit. If you build a new ground, you're going to take on a huge amount of debt; it's a distraction from the main issue of getting the core business going.

'I wouldn't like to share with Arsenal, but I might have considered it on the basis that there was a north London stadium and the two clubs share it. But now, they've got a huge debt, and it's gonna kill Arsenal. It might not kill them this year but it'll kill them at some stage and we've just got to wait for them to die. The fact the club are even talking to Arsenal is just fucking madness. If it was the other way round and we had a huge debt, you can't imagine David Dein banging on our door offering to bail us out. It's a non-runner. Football in the twentieth century was one way and it might be different in the twenty-first, but this, I just don't see the need.

'Arsenal played at Wembley and didn't like it, and when they opened the new Clock End, Spurs fans trashed it, so there's that aspect to consider too. There's the whole thing about home advantage, which would go. And when you go to Spurs and you go to the Bricklayer's Arms before the game, the guvnor's got all Spurs programmes on the wall. If it was a shared stadium, what would the pubs do? Have reversible programmes? It's all a bit, well, it's all about the money rather than the football club.'

With the club once again rushing to embrace transition, Jim's website remains a vital port of call for many fans who want to get a handle on what's going on. So is Jim confident he can continue the flow of reliable tips, such as being the first to flag up the signing of Robbie Keane? He admits his contacts vary in quality.

'There's a lot of rubbish but some people have just emerged,' he says. 'Some have turned out to be quite good sources with various connections, and I also get to know about the rumours that are going round in the north London Jewish community from people who know people.'

There's fun to be had from the ever-turning rumour mill, as Jim found out when rumours that Spurs were about to sign Real

Madrid's Fernando Morientes began to circulate. 'I did get a tip before the whole thing broke that Levy was going out to see Morientes, so I dropped a little clue on. I knew his birthday was 5 April – 5/4 is a betting price and it's known in the trade as "wrist" because when bookies signal to each other, this price is signified by touching the wrist.

'So I put "Levy's going to meet birthday wrist and he might sign." People went absolutely mad on all the message boards trying to guess who he was; it was quite funny. Especially the number of people who thought it was Hasselbaink – wrist being a wanker!'

There's also a growing role as an unofficial host for visiting Spurs fans that Jim's happy to continue. 'Being an internationalist and all that, I put up a welcome in all the different languages, and people get in contact,' he explains. 'I've been amazed at supporters' clubs like the Tottenhams Venner – 3,000 members in Norway, as well as in Sweden and Denmark – and the people in Malta, Singapore and, of course, my friends in Cork, Republic of Ireland. When they come over, I look out for them. There's also Cumbrian Spurs, who come down on a big coach, and they're great when we go up there, finding pubs and that. Every game there'll be somebody coming across. It's quite good, you'll meet them in the pub and show them round.'

Of the many good times he's had following Spurs, one still takes pride of place. 'For the 1981 Cup final replay, because we lived so close to Wembley we went down there on the Sunday and got three tickets,' he says. 'We were sitting just above the Royal Box and we had a brilliant view. The thing with me dad, he wasn't the most enthusiastic supporter, cheering and stuff like that, but as Ricky [Villa] was doing his run he was the first bloke in that stadium on our side to stand up. I couldn't believe it – his arms in the air even before Ricky had scored. I'd never seen me dad do that before, or since.

'Afterwards, we all went to the bit where the players' tunnel is and we thought we'd watch the coaches as they come out. And then Graham Roberts appeared, so we went over there and Roberts had his medal with him. Dad was talking to someone and I got chatting to Roberts. The top of the Cup was like this horrible hat, they used to wear it on their heads, and cheekily I asked, "Can I have your hat, Graham?", and he just plonked it on me head. Well, I couldn't believe it. I got to touch his medal, and we had a couple of words.

'Now, every time I look at that photograph of Perryman holding the Cup I think, "I got that." It was quite good that the old man went up there. I would never have thought of doing something like that.'

8

We're the Shelf Side: Danny the Drum

We're the Shelf Side
We're the Shelf Side
We're the Shelf Side, Tottenham

The first Saturday of January 2004 meant the FA Cup third round, and this season's campaign seemed to offer Spurs some respite from their wretched League run with a home draw against Crystal Palace. But with Spurs in the form they were, and Palace on a run under new manager Iain Dowie, this had the makings of that great football cliché, the potential banana skin. To add to Tottenham's problems, top scorer Freddie Kanouté had broken the news that he would be away at the African Nations Cup for up to five weeks. The news that their 'Frenchman' was, in fact, from Mali came as a surprise to both fans and the club. Freddie had played for the French Under-21s, but a recent rule change meant that he was eligible to play for the country his father was born in.

Predictably, Tottenham handled the affair badly – making their irritation clear and putting public pressure on Freddie to stay. David Pleat surpassed himself with some ill-judged comments and outright ignorance, referring to Samoa, in one rambling contribution about international football, as 'Samosa', before the club finally realised it wouldn't be able to bully its player out of the decision he had taken. Fans were divided too, although his decision didn't appear to have set many against him as they greeted him with cheers at the Palace game. Freddie did himself no harm at all by grabbing a hat-trick against a limited Palace side as Spurs won without breaking sweat.

The visit of Birmingham City four days later posed a greater threat. The Blues had one of the most solid defences in the Premiership, were challenging for a European spot and had beaten Spurs on the opening day. But they were routed by a Tottenham side which welcomed back Simon Davies and witnessed a virtuoso performance from Stephane Dalmat. Birmingham were hit by injuries, but a 4–1 victory was still just what was needed. A good week was rounded off with a dour 1–0 win at Leeds, and while victories against a weak First Division side, an injury-ridden Premier team and another in freefall needed to be looked at in perspective, any run of wins would do.

As Freddie Kanouté jetted off to Africa – he and Spurs now apparently all friends again – a thought-provoking article appeared in *The Independent*. In it, a source close to Daniel Levy insisted he had a new manager under contract, a top name who would be coming in the summer but whose identity had to remain secret. Many fans were calling for the appointment of a manager as soon as possible, but the board had previously announced that David Pleat and Chris Hughton would stay until the end of the season. To many, this seemed the worst of all worlds, with the uncertainty that would result from not knowing what was coming next undermining the morale of current squad members and making signing new players almost impossible. The article appeared to be an attempt by the club to convince the doubters it was determined to appoint the right manager in the right way, but it also contained an astonishing assertion that, if correct, would cast further doubt on the competence of those running Tottenham.

The board's biggest regret, it was said, was the sacking of George Graham. If this was true, it would mean that, as many suspected, Graham was sacked not because of the official explanation of poor decisions or breaching confidences, but because the new board wanted to play to the gallery and sack a manager whom the fans detested.

A few days later, the same journalist, Jason Burt, ran another story in which a club source had apparently said that planning permission for expanding the East Stand had been refused. But the club had previously said it did have planning permission, but was waiting for the transport issues to be resolved before proceeding. Were the goalposts being moved in order to move the entire ground? The article was headlined 'Spurs' desire is to share with Arsenal'.

Of far more immediate concern to most fans was the feverish

speculation about the identity of the new manager. While Martin O'Neill had long been considered the 'number one target' whom the board insisted it would get, it was rumoured that the Celtic manager wasn't keen on working with Pleat, who had been told his job as Director of Football was safe whatever happened. The latest name to emerge was that of Italy's national coach Giovanni Trapattoni. Then Wales manager Mark Hughes was rumoured to be coming as Trap's assistant, and as the month progressed even England manager Sven-Goran Eriksson's name was being seriously talked about as Levy's mystery man.

But there was no escaping the fact that poor form and a lack of application on the pitch were mirrored by cock-ups, bickering, recriminations and suspicion off it. With Enic's much-vaunted five-year plan in disarray, many supporters took the view that the club had reached a new low – worse even than the relegation year of 1977, because the gap between Spurs and the current 'big three' was widening almost day by day.

Unsurprisingly, fans were left bewildered and angry. How had the club with such a depth of support, charging among the highest ticket prices in the country, been allowed to decline to such a degree?

Spending money was clearly not the problem. Both Alan Sugar and Daniel Levy had sanctioned one of the biggest cumulative outlays in the ten years of the Premiership – well in excess of £100 million and surpassing the net spending of Arsenal, who in the same period had won the Double twice, the FA Cup on a further two occasions, a European trophy and a League Cup.

Tottenham have not been alone in spending vast sums without reward. Newcastle, Manchester City and, of course, Leeds had also spent big and risked big, with varying degrees of success, but, by what fans regard as the really important measure of what constitutes a return on investment, only one of those four had lifted a trophy in the last decade – and that was Spurs.

For a club with the size of expectations of Tottenham, however, picking up the odd scrap that more successful clubs toss aside is simply not good enough. At the close of 2003, Arsenal were unbeaten domestically and through to the quarter-finals of the Champions League. By contrast, Spurs had lost 11 League games, were out of the Carling Cup and unlikely to qualify for European football. *Plus ça change* . . .

For all this, Spurs were still attracting crowds of 30,000 plus – not bad for a bunch of fickle fans – although the atmosphere after kick-off was often subdued and nervous.

Indeed, the issue of atmosphere at football grounds is one that most exercises supporters. Talk to any football fan whose matchday experience harks back to the time before the beginning of the Premier League and it is likely they will wistfully recall the age when games had real atmosphere. Not the phoney, 'clash-of-the-titans' exaggeration that accompanies all too many over-hyped modern encounters, but a time when crowds sang, cheered, shouted and roared (with abuse as much as encouragement and celebration) and didn't need Robbie Williams blaring out over the PA to generate some volume.

The nostalgia for the noisy, fervent crowds of yesteryear provides a glaring contrast with the often lifeless, passionless mood of the modern British football game. Whether it's the frequently ridiculed Highbury Library, Cold Trafford or the soporific hush of Snoozecastle, all too often games are played out before mute audiences who can rarely be bothered to raise an eyebrow, let alone a cheer. The advent of the contemporary football stadium has brought relative comfort and security – but at the cost of excitement and noise.

Tottenham Hotspur's ground can also be a depressingly sterile place. Dubbed Quiet Hart Lane for its occasionally lifeless atmosphere, the often sullen mood of the Spurs home crowd has mirrored the bland fare that successive teams have served up.

There are, however, some occasions when the supporters rise from their collective slumber and produce an atmosphere worthy of the name. Instrumental in this are the fans who for decades have been responsible for conducting the crowd's support. They are largely unknown but not unsung: it is their homespun chants that are taken up as club anthems, often imbued with a wit and lyrical flourish that a poet would be proud of. No one knows for certain who these terrace bards are – who was the first Spurs fan who sang 'Glory, Glory Hallelujah', for instance?

Of late, Spurs fans have been reduced in the main to singing songs that deride their near-neighbours. In recent years, however, there has emerged another kind of crowd agitator – one who literally bangs the drum for the Tottenham cause.

Danny Spalding is his name, but most know him appropriately

enough as Danny the Drum. He can be found at every home game, perched on the middle tier in the East Stand towards the Park Lane end. The location is no accident: this was the site of the Shelf and the Cage, the two areas of terracing from where most of White Hart Lane's atmosphere originated, before the introduction of an all-seater stadium. It is here that Danny beats out a regular rhythm to stir the home crowd into life.

'The reaction it gets is unbelievable,' says Danny, a born-and-bred Tottenhamite now living in Hertfordshire. 'I'm not sure if it's fame necessarily; maybe it's made me infamous. But I've had such brilliant experiences with it. It's not about who it is banging the drum, but my name just goes well with it. Word has got around on websites and that, with people saying, "Oh yeah, I know that geezer", but it could be anybody doing it, to be honest, it's the drum that is well known.'

To be equally honest, the drum is not to everybody's taste – 'that poxy drum' being one of the less kind comments from some rival supporters – but with a need for less orthodox means to inspire a bit of enthusiasm among apathetic fans, Danny has no qualms about taking on the responsibility.

'I can't take the actual credit for the drum in the first place because it was someone else who actually started taking it, a fella called Gary Spize. He used to do it sporadically, until he never turned up with it at all. Me and my mates noticed that he wasn't doing it any more, which we thought was a shame, because it would work so well in getting the crowd going, so we thought one of us should take it over. So it just ended up with me buying the drum, and that was about 1996. It was partly because we were getting fed up with the lack of atmosphere.'

For years, that absence of atmosphere had troubled many a Spurs follower, not just because it meant the crowd were not encouraging the players to a great enough degree (in the often vain hope that they would then produce some football worth cheering) but also because it devalued the matchday experience for the fan. Danny is simply a dedicated, loyal supporter who had had enough of watching games that lacked the excitement they used to have.

He remembers his initial exposure to a football crowd as 'unbelievable, just unbelievable. This was during the early '70s so there was a lot of trouble then. I remember my dad taking me and one of my mates and standing on the Shelf. West Ham got into the bottom of the terracing and there was a bit of a fracas. But I was with my dad and felt safe, and I just remember how great the atmosphere was – thousands and thousands of people standing up and shouting, cheering and singing, which you just don't get any more.'

Like many of his contemporaries, Danny lays the blame for that lack of atmosphere at the door of all-seater stadia. Few could deny the need for wholesale changes after the Hillsborough disaster finally exposed the scandal of decrepit, badly managed grounds that for decades had offered next to nothing in the way of safety and security. (Tottenham supporters in particular have good reason to remember just how dangerous supposedly 'first-class' grounds were. In the 1981 FA Cup semi-final against Wolves played at Hillsborough, a disaster was only averted when fans from Spurs crammed into the notorious Leppings Lane end spilled on to the track area in front of the stand.)

No fan with a modicum of sense wants to return to those dark days, and Danny is no exception. But he speaks for many when he bemoans the climate of silent indifference that now plagues many grounds.

'The atmosphere has never been right since they introduced all-seaters. I don't know what it's like at other grounds, but, in the old days, when you could move around the ground, it was better. To my mind the atmosphere started to suffer when the away fans could have the Park Lane end, and we had the Paxton and the Shelf. What happened was that the away fans could out-shout us because of the echo coming from under the roof of the Park Lane. When all-seaters came in, well, that was it really.

'I can remember one game against West Ham and there was definitely 50,000 in there, and that's in the '80s before they put the seating in. And I can remember coming away from the ground and thinking, "That was absolutely brilliant." Not just the game but the whole experience – the noise, the excitement, the atmosphere. It just isn't what it used to be.'

Some might argue that such complaints have more to do with the general lack of excitement on the pitch at Spurs in recent years. It's a point that Danny concedes. 'Our atmosphere is not as good as at some grounds, but in my opinion the excitement comes from two things. If we was in a relegation battle, the crowd would respond to that and show a bit more spirit – that would create an atmosphere.

'If we was winning the League, winning trophies and stuff, I think that would create a euphoria. I think our atmosphere suffers 'cos we're a midtable side going neither one way or the other. If you was to look at any club in the same position and go round their ground, you'd find the same problem.

'You go to Wolves at Molineux – great atmosphere, but you know that they're gonna be relegated so they are determined to enjoy their season in the Premiership. But that's partly why I started with the drum. It's my view that over a period of years we just began to accept things the way they were, but once that drum gets going it lifts the crowd. I remember one game against Chelsea [the 2002 League Cup semi-final], for the whole of the second half, 45 minutes, everybody was singing "Glenn Hoddle's blue and white army" – the whole ground, even in the West Stand, in the prawn-sandwich seats. That was in a ground with all seating and it was directly down to the drum.

'But it's difficult to bang the drum all the time because people become reliant on it. I don't beat it all the time now, I only do it when I think there's a bit of a lull. So, to be honest, I'm not sure if it's a positive or a negative thing.'

Judging by the reaction he gets, it's safe to assume most fans view Danny as doing a worthwhile service for the club. Danny has had no official response from the club, but has no problems taking the drum into White Hart Lane; former acting chairman David Buchler even paid for a replacement after some particularly eager thumping resulted in a split drum skin. It's also a struggle for Danny to carry his unique matchday accessory. 'It's bloody hard carrying the drum with all those people around and getting in your way,' he says wearily.

There are compensations, though: 'I was going down Tottenham High Road and this bird sees me and starts coming towards me. She virtually jumps on me and says, "Oh, I love you" like a proper nutter, and she was a stunner as well. She's with her old man, but she goes, "I know it sounds really silly but do you mind if I kiss you?" So I said, "Go on then". Honestly, it's mad, it's like I'm getting groupies now!

'Another experience that springs to mind with me was when we all knew in our hearts that Sol Campbell was on his way out. He was injured and he was coming through the main gate before one game, wearing his suit and this little kid was going for his autograph. What happened was that I went past and this kid goes, "Dad, Dad, it's the drum, the man with the drum!" and he's grabbed the programme out of Sol Campbell's hand as he's signing it and run over to me going, "Can I have your autograph?" I said, "No, you don't want my autograph", but the kid looked genuinely sad so I thought, "Ah, sod it", and I got into the part, do you know what I mean? So I wrote in it: "Best wishes, Dan the Drum". Campbell's looked over and I've given him a little wry smile and thought, "Yeah, 1–0".'

Mention of the past club captain yet again raises the issue of loyalty and the bitter antipathy towards former heroes. When it comes to Campbell, a few Spurs fans have settled into a near-permanent state of resentment, their anger acting as a distraction to more immediate concerns of the club. Others simply want to put it all behind them and consign the whole sorry saga to history.

Unfortunately, that has been made more difficult by the player's own revisiting of the dispute. When Danny was interviewed, Campbell had just released an autobiographical DVD in which the Arsenal defender spoke about his 'hurt' at the way he was treated at Tottenham, making criticisms against Spurs fans.

Danny Spalding is as easy-going a football fan as you could wish to meet, but say the name 'Campbell' and his mood visibly sinks.

'I've met Sol Campbell subsequent to him doing the dirty on us. About two years ago, it was in Tesco's in Hertford. I went up to him and I went, "Sol, can I have a quick word with you?" He went, "Move along!" And I went, "I beg your pardon?"

'He wouldn't talk to me. I said to him, "All I want to do is ask you something. I'm not a nutter. My name's Danny. I do the drum up on the Shelf, you know who I am. We can do this sensibly, all I want to do is ask you a couple of questions." But he wouldn't have none of it, he just ignored me. I admit then I did lose my rag. I said to him: "Do you know that I've got a boy of six and I'm trying to teach him about loyalty. He thought you was the best thing since sliced bread, our club captain, you were a hero to him, but look what you done."

'When we've lost to Arsenal, my boy Alfie has been given sympathy cards; when Glenn got the sack, he cried. I'm not joking. So I said to Campbell, "Do you realise what you've done to my boy, how you've let him down?" But he wasn't having any of it and he just ignored me.'

That Campbell chose to ignore his accuser is hardly surprising in an era when players have genuine fears for their own personal safety. Danny is not the violent type, but his frustration – even despair – is tangible. His is a problem any number of mums and dads who support any club outside of the current 'big three' have: how to prevent the apples of their eyes forgoing the family tradition and falling under the aggressively marketed spell of Manchester United, Arsenal and the like. Danny has faced just such a dilemma.

'Alfie's been going to games with me since he was three, but he hasn't seen any success with Spurs, though I've always tried to tell him about the importance of staying loyal, staying loyal to the club. Anyway, one day he came home and says to me, "Dad, can I have a David Beckham shirt?" He didn't specifically ask for a Man Utd shirt; it was the *name* he wanted, regardless of the team.

'I told him to go to his room, sit down for ten minutes and think about it and then come back and tell me why he shouldn't have a Beckham shirt. He comes back and says, "It's because we're Spurs – we're loyal." In the end we made a deal and I got him an England shirt with Beckham on it.'

There will no doubt be non-football fans who wince at such parental insistence, arguing that, in the final analysis, football is still only a game. They are correct, of course, but it is a pointless exercise trying to reason the unreasonable with non-fans and convey just how important football is to its devotees.

In recent years, Tottenham's lack of success and the trophy hauls of Arsenal, Chelsea and Manchester United have caused a breakdown in local loyalties that would have been unthinkable 20 years ago, a phenomenon Danny is all too aware of.

'When you went up the A10, through towns like Cheshunt, Broxbourne, Hertford, they were Tottenham places – it was always traditionally Spurs. I still drink in Broxbourne and it is heavily Spurs, but you go out to Hertford now and you see kids playing football, like my kid, who plays for Hertford Town Youth, when the kids turn up for training they're wearing their club shirts and there's more Arsenal than Spurs. I think that's a damn shame. It's 'cos they're more successful, simple as that.

'I want my son to experience the happiness I've had with Spurs. The 1981 FA Cup replay for one. I was living in Walthamstow at the time. I was 13. I couldn't get to the replay, but I just remember the whole day – planning where you were going to watch it, seeing such an amazing game and then that goal – well, even now I get goosebumps just thinking about it.

'Even when we won the Worthington Cup in '99, that was great – celebrations when you win something, there's nothing like it. After 1991, I drove home on top of some fella's roof from Wembley and we thought, "How long can we stay on?", but we drove all the way back to Tottenham, and they'd shut off the High Road because there were so many people out celebrating.

'It's all changed now, though. I do a lot of work through north London and I'm up in Tottenham a lot. It's all changed, but when there's a big game, it's like being a child again. I know so many people through Spurs and when you go from pub to pub on a matchday and you see all the people you know, many from the old days, it's great. Before the game that's almost more important than the game. Being in that atmosphere, that's like the old Tottenham.'

Unlike many Spurs fans who have no real association with Tottenham the area, for Danny his sense of identity with this often-maligned little corner of north London is vitally important.

'It does matter very much to me. One of the proudest things I've got is having "Tottenham" in my passport as my place of birth and it's in my driving licence. I'd like to move back there – but not in the state it's in now. A road sign of White Hart Lane N17 might do, though. But, yes, I'm proud, very proud.'

Danny is carrying on a paternal tradition of supporting Spurs. His first exposure to the club came about through his dad's weekend work. Living close to the ground in Lordship Lane, the father-and-son team sold unofficial merchandise. 'To be fair, as kids we were always quite hard up. My dad was scratching around a bit trying to make a living. What he did was sell football souvenirs, rosettes and that kind of thing, that was his sideline and I used to go round with him as a kid.

'So I got a good appreciation of following football in that way. It was always going to be Spurs. For the FA Cup final, my dad would always go and sell rosettes for whoever was the underdog team at their end of the ground, such as Ipswich when they beat Arsenal in '78. So as a kid you sort of got swept along with that, but Spurs were always my team, always. I was born in Tottenham and my dad was a season-ticket holder, so it's a hereditary thing really.

'I went to loads of grounds, actually, but never went in them – mostly around London. We never went up north because for some reason they never bought rosettes. I still have a half-crown that Bobby Moore gave to me when my mum had to deliver some stuff to the West Ham shop. I was only about three and don't remember too much about it, but she said he had plenty of time for us.'

Danny graduated to going to games with his mates, coinciding with the early 1980s fashion when no self-respecting fan would be seen dead in anything but designer sports labels ('I was definitely a Casual and it mattered *very* much the clothes I wore!'). He rarely travelled to away games, work commitments as an alarm security technician requiring him to be on call and within easy reach of London at weekends.

Danny's phone rings. It's a mate talking about all things Spurs and the need to get behind the team, a key role for Danny – the man with the drum. They chat about the positive effect it had on a game earlier in the season, immediately after Glenn Hoddle's sacking, which he elaborates on when the call ends.

'I don't mind not winning the League year in, year out. I want to see good football but I dunno, maybe we've been starved a bit, but for the Everton game we came out really up for it and it was brilliant – a smile on everyone's face. There was some nice one-touch football, Kanouté scoring a cracker and I thought, "Hold on – that's what I come to Spurs for, 30-yard rasper in the top corner – lovely; Robbie Keane nutmegging people, that's what I want."'

One thing Danny does not want is the phenomenon of the 'new' football fan to continue. A man who passionately believes in the need for an atmosphere at football grounds, there's no doubting what his thoughts are concerning the new breed of supporter, for whom getting behind the team means a polite ripple of applause and increasing his or her equity in the club's PLC parent company.

'If the truth be known, I'd soon get all these "Oh, yes, ra-ra-ra!" Islingtonites out. Listen, I go to rugby 'cos my business partner is a rugby man and I've been to Twickenham a couple of times. Now I hate football hooliganism, I really do, and so to see what all these fans at the rugby say about French and English fans mixing together, it's very nice. But, not being funny, I don't want to sing the French national anthem. I want a bit of hostility and rivalry, you know!

'Half my family are Arsenal 'cos my mum's side come from Balls

Pond Road. There's some lovely banter between us. When we lose to Arsenal, which, as you know, happens all too often, I get wreaths from Interflora laid at the door with "deepest sympathies" and all that. It's good banter, I like that. I'd never want to see Arsenal go out of the top division.

'These sort of things are getting lost with the money and the way football's changed 'cos of the new kind of support. When you hear Gooners these days saying the Spurs game isn't so important to them any more, that's bollocks. It's 'cos they're relatively new fans with their Islington Upper Street lah-di-dah-ness – and they don't know what it all means.'

9

If you know your history: Chris Kaufman and Jeremy Dear

It's a grand old team to play for
It's a grand old team to see
And if you know your history
It's enough to make your heart go whoooo
We don't care what the other teams say
What the hell do we care?
'Cos we only know
That there's gonna be a show
And the Tottenham Hotspur will be there

As January drew to a close, the extraordinary general meeting of the club's shareholders at which Daniel Levy hoped his cunning convertible preference shares plan would be backed loomed and arguments raged among ordinary fans about the pros and cons of the scheme. Whatever happened to discussing who should play on the wing?

Levy's scheme certainly looked suspicious, and bore all the hallmarks of a man for whom the phrase 'too clever by half' was almost a personal motto. However, the alternative proposed by the rebels was to raise a £15 million loan, and more debt was not an attractive option.

As debate grew ever more heated, Levy gave an interview to PA's Neil Silver in which he claimed the bigger shareholding for Enic was 'a consequence of the issue, not our motive'. He also warned: 'If this fundraising does not go through it throws doubt on whether there will be any activity from us in the January window and without doubt it will have an impact on the quality of manager we have in mind.' Coupled with the fact that he had promised 'major changes' in January, Levy's line was crystal clear – his was the only game in town and failure to back him would damage Spurs.

As the spat unfolded, it was also revealed that David Sullivan, the proprietor of Birmingham City FC, owned a stake in Tottenham. His opposition to the scheme enabled Levy to strengthen his assertion that the rebels were out to damage Tottenham, but many asked how it was that the owner of one football club could be allowed to hold a significant stake in a rival. Another example of football's warped economics.

The intrigue was forgotten for a moment as an impressive Spurs beat Liverpool 2–1 at home. It was a significant game for Helder Postiga, the young striker already being labelled a flop after his £6 million move to Tottenham, as he finally bagged his first Premiership goal.

Spurs had now won four games on the bounce since the New Year. At the EGM, Levy won his vote, then made a statement that emphasised just why so many fans found it difficult to take anything he said at face value. 'I very much hope that fans will see a strengthening of the squad in the summer,' he said. 'We do not have a great deal of time left in this transfer window, but we are still working on several deals.' The contrast with his words before the vote – 'If this fundraising does not go through it throws doubt on whether there will be any activity from us in the January window' – could not have been clearer.

With all the internal machinations, factional fights and grass-roots organisation, supporting Tottenham Hotspur can sometimes seem more like an episode from a political drama than sporting entertainment. So it's perhaps no surprise to hear that, alongside the showbiz personalities more usually identified as the club's high-profile support, there's a sizeable Spurs following among the ranks of Britain's trade unions and political parties.

Ask anyone to describe a typical football fan, let alone a typical Spurs fan, and it's a fair bet they won't describe either Chris Kaufman or Jeremy Dear. Chris, 57, is National Secretary for Public Services in the TGWU, the country's biggest union, while Jeremy is head of the media union the NUJ, at 37 the youngest General Secretary in the TUC.

When anyone from the world of politics lets their footballing allegiance be known, it tends to create the suspicion that there's a bandwagon being jumped on, a legacy of Tony Blair's infamous efforts to convince football fans he was 'one of us' and the remarkable speed with which MPs of all parties rushed to parade their colours after so many years when admitting you liked football was considered political death. But Spurs, more renowned for high-profile showbiz and media fans like Bruce Forsyth, Kenneth Branagh, Richard Littlejohn and Danny Kelly, can also boast a healthy long-term following in the upper reaches of the Labour and trade-union movements – dedication to the blue and white of Spurs seems to run deeper on the red half of the political spectrum.

Chris Kaufman can remember his first game 49 years ago. 'It was 1955 against Boston United in the Cup. It must have been the third round. I went with my dad or my dad's friends, and I only saw the ball when it was kicked about 20 yards in the air, but I was hooked. It was just as well because if you didn't stick up for Spurs where I lived then you got thrown in the pond. I grew up in Hackney, and went to school just up the road from Stoke Newington.

'It cost about a penny ha'penny to go down to Spurs on the 149 bus. The first time I used to pay to get in it was nine old pence as a junior, then I remember getting chips when we came out. Fourpence for a normal bag or sixpence for a big bag from Young Sam's, it was, on that corner where the Red Lion is, near Bruce Grove.

'For years I carried on getting in for half price as a junior, until one day the doorman said, "Are you trying to get in as a pensioner?"

'I used to go with a pal called Mick Finer, who was about half my size, and so for him I would push down to the front. You're talking late '50s/early '60s now, when Spurs had become really successful, huge crowds, and we'd turn up at least an hour before to get a decent view. As you came in you'd be confronted by a complete wall of bodies, and it'd look as if it was impossible to get through. But being old hands we knew we could. I'd wait until there was a little chink of light somewhere, and we'd just shove an arm in. That'd make a bit of a breach in the wall, and we'd begin to get through.

'Because we always stood on the same part, there were these fellas, we used to call 'em Methuselah and his mates. One time Maurice Norman, who was the Spurs centre-half, had a real ding-dong battle with Derek Kevan, the West Brom centre-forward – we later found

Derek was a T&G member working in a warehouse, and we put him in the T&G paper – but this day it was two huge men tussling for the ball, neither of them would give an inch, and they came chasing over. Norman just gave him a little nudge as they got to the edge, and Kevan came about eight foot into the crowd. I remember this vividly, this fella behind me said [deadpan], "I see Maurice is lashing out," and the one next to him said, "Maurice lashing out", and the third one said exactly the same thing. They used to have these little bons mots going backwards and forwards. I can see 'em now.'

Chris has never lost the bug, but the matchday experience now is very different from when he started going.

'I still haven't got used to the idea of sitting down. I feel it's like being at the theatre. You've really got to be standing up to watch a football match. That's why, if I get a chance, I go to Leyton Orient now, because . . . obviously you are participating if you're sitting down, but you don't feel like you are.'

The way the crowd shows its support has also changed. 'I can't remember orchestrated singing in the very early days. I first became aware of singing at Spurs during those European nights, maybe during the year they won the Double. I know that whole "Glory, Glory Hallelujah" business came around that time. I was at that game when Spurs beat Gornik 8–1. In the first tie we'd gone four goals down, and we'd managed to nick a couple of goals back. I remember such a wall of sound from the Spurs fans when they came out that the Polish players were physically diminished, they were white. I can't imagine what it must've been like for them. I'd never known such an intensity of noise. Spurs just completely obliterated them, 8–1.'

That Spurs team had already gone down in history as the first to win the modern domestic Double of League Championship and FA Cup in the same season, but Chris remembers it was a very low-key start to the Double season as far as the supporters were concerned.

'First of all, there wasn't all this pre-season hype. The only pre-season game was the first team against the second team, and nobody bothered with that. I didn't see the first game of the season, but I remember it was 2–0, Spurs against Everton. It was 0–0 for a long time and then towards the end they popped a couple of goals in. And I don't think anybody thought too much about that, but gradually as you began to see these other teams playing, you began to realise that something extraordinary was going on.

'They evolved during that season. Once they got that string of 11 games winning, then 17 unbeaten I think it was, you just never expected to lose. You went to every game expecting a win. That's why it's so hard on our children, because they haven't seen any success like that. In those days you just expected to lord it over everybody. Even the Arsenal. I went to the Arsenal game at Highbury and Spurs didn't have Smudger Smith, they put on Frankie Saul, who was just 17. And he scored! It just seemed like whatever they wanted to do, they could do. It was just in such style, a kind of a mixture of the push-and-run, which they'd done in the '50s, with individual skills as well. Somebody like Cliff Jones, he wouldn't have fitted into the '50s team, he ran with the ball. But he was such an extraordinary player, he was only a tiny little bloke but he could jump higher than people a foot taller than him, and he was as brave as any of 'em.'

As the excitement really did begin to build, disaster struck for Chris.

'I broke my leg at Easter playing football at school, so I missed the run-in to the Double. I would have been there for the Sheffield Wednesday game, which is when they wrapped it up, but instead I was lying on the bed with my foot up in the air. And of course there was no big coverage on TV then. But luckily I could watch the Cup final.'

He may have missed his side's crowning moment, but Chris recognises he was very lucky to get hooked on football just as his team were sweeping all before them, and he treasures the memories of the time.

'Probably the most amazing game that I saw was Spurs 10 Everton 4 – Nicholson's first game. The players didn't know what had happened; we didn't know he'd taken over as manager because there wasn't all that hype that there is now. They were 6–1 up at half-time and then they got an injury, so they were playing with ten men. An Everton player got a hat-trick but ended up on the losing side.

'And there was a game against Burnley, in the Double season. I always used to leave just before the end, to beat the crowds. I always get annoyed when football commentators complain about that, because they're all mollycoddled. People make arrangements beforehand about meeting outside and if you don't get away early you're going to be there for an extra couple of hours. Anyway, Spurs went four up, and Burnley were a brilliant team, Spurs played 'em off the park, real flair but a lot of punch as well. They were no pushovers. People like Terry Dyson and Dave Mackay and Smudger Smith, they would duff people up – but in a gentle sort of way [laughs] – you ought to have been privileged to be duffed up by such a team, you know! Burnley got one back just before half-time, and then blow me if it didn't end up 4–4. It was a most incredible game. Both teams played out of their skin. We had to leave, even at 4–4, so for all I knew it could've ended up 6–4, but it didn't. But it was tremendous entertainment.'

In the early 1960s, journeys by large numbers of fans to away games were less common, and Chris was no different in limiting his trips on the road.

'We didn't travel often. I used to go to the London games, and I used to go to Chelsea home games with a mate, even in the days before Greaves had started, and I used to go to Fulham home games, just 'cos I had mates who used to go. The only reason I would've gone to Arsenal would be to see them lose.

'Outside London the first one that I went to was away to Ipswich in the year after Spurs had won the Double. I went on the supporters' coach, and it sticks in my mind because it's the one that if Spurs had won they'd have won the double Double. Ipswich was a real kind of rustic setting and it was a lovely pitch, rumoured to be the best, and very enclosed. Alf Ramsey had 'em playing quite a rustic game, there was some skill there as well, but the tactics were pretty direct, around this Ted Phillips, "Thunderball" Ted Phillips.

'Spurs were playing some good stuff, they went a goal up, and they could've got a good few more. Then towards half-time Ted Phillips got the ball somewhere near the halfway line and he booted it into the net. It was quite brutally uncomplicated, and suddenly the whole place . . . well, the roof lifted off and suddenly it was conceivable that Spurs might not win. Up till then it was just a question of how much they'd win by and what sort of exhibition they'd put on for the locals. This uncomplicated hoofing of the ball into the net was a very rude awakening. But it ignited the crowd and in the second half they carried on where they'd left off, and Ted Phillips, he did it again. I can remember Cliff Jones doing all these arabesques and Les Allen interchanging, but it just wasn't working. I think they ended up winning 3–1. On the coach getting back there was lots of catcalls from all the local people. We were still sauntering around saying, "Wait till we get you back at White Hart Lane, we'll show you what's what."

'So we lost at Tottenham as well! If they'd won just one of those, they'd've won the League and won the double Double. So I do remember that one well.'

Every supporter can remember their own 'Glory Days' but for most, life moves on and situations change.

'I carried on going until the mid- to late 1960s,' says Chris, 'and then I went on to Brighton, to college. I'd still come up for the odd game, but I wouldn't come up so often. I met my wife, Pieta, in 1972 and I took her along to a few games. She knew nothing about football and still doesn't, but I used to lure her along on the grounds that it was exciting. She never saw Spurs score a goal the whole time she was there, or at least she claims she didn't. They must have hit a bad spell, so she's never been particularly taken with Spurs, and I had to be a bit selective about the games I could go to. Probably what saved me was the children coming along. Now we've got a majority in the house for watching football. Both the children, Kieran and Sophie, he's now 17 and she's now 19, they've been going since they were 7. So whenever there's a rumpus about what's on the television, being democrats we have a vote on it and we normally come out on top. And we're members and we go about once a month, or sometimes I'm able to scrounge a ticket some other how.'

Chris was soon playing an active role in the trade-union movement, which put further pressure on weekends.

'There used to be clashes, but normally I managed to find ways round them,' he laughs. 'If there were conferences, you'd have to miss out. I remember going to a conference in Ipswich where I was the speaker and I got off the train and I found there was a huge number of people following me. I thought, "Bloody hell, there's been some good publicity for this meeting." But I turned round after going past the football ground and they'd all gone in to Portman Road!'

One of Chris's most vivid memories is the day he took a delegation of foreign trade-union officials to the World Famous Home of the Spurs.

'They were Russians, some East Germans as well, but mainly Russians. In my family there's quite a few people that speak Russian, with my sister being an interpreter and my wife teaching it, so I got talked in to taking this delegation to Spurs v. Aston Villa. On this occasion we did actually get seats, to make sure everyone got in, so I was already feeling a bit odd.

'It was in the days when Spurs had this Laurie Brown. They got him off the Arsenal, which always proves to be a bad move. It works for them – they get our best players, but we never get anything out of theirs. It's counter-productive, and Laurie Brown is a case in point. He was bought as the new John Charles, who could play both centre-half and centre-forward. John Charles was supreme at both, but Laurie Brown was awful at both. They had him playing centre-half against Aston Villa. But at the beginning of the game it was all Spurs attacking and by half-time they were 5–1 up. Then Aston Villa got it back to 5–2, and then I noticed that every time Laurie Brown went anywhere near the ball the whole Spurs defence fell into a kind of collective St Vitus Dance-cum-nervous breakdown. Suddenly we looked about to cave in.

'It went to 5–3 and I could see things were looking a bit grim so I said to one of the blokes leading the delegation, "I think we ought to start heading towards the exit." But he said, "No, no. It is a very good game. You've told me Spurs is the best in the world, and I can see they play very good football."

'So we stuck around, and it went to 5–4, the ball bounced off Laurie Brown's ankle straight into the path of one of their forwards. So I got up and I said, "Look, this is how we do it in England, we should go", because I knew what would happen, being a Spurs supporter.

'And lo, that is what happened. I think Laurie Brown got the ball and he just had to pass it out and he gave it to some Villa player, there was a little exchange of passes and the ball ended up in the Spurs net. By that time there was no point in me saying go or not go. It was excruciating for me, but the Russians thought it was wonderful. But that's what being a Spurs supporter is about.

'On the other hand, I can remember a cup game against Burnley when they were 3–1 down and ended up winning 4–3, Gilzean got a couple, so it can happen the other way.'

Of the many changes Chris has seen, the rise of hooliganism is the one he regrets most.

'I didn't get involved in any of the punch-ups. It never put me off, but I did think it was unpleasant and crude, the name-calling, the racism. That would've been the early '70s. But you knew enough not to get involved. It certainly was getting more and more lumpen, it wasn't something you felt proud of. I used to feel proud of the crowd, which had the power to change things, because that's what trade unions do, that's what socialists want. You didn't feel that with a mob going round punching each other's lights out, generally in a cowardly sort of way.

'And there were the racist chants as well. Maybe calling it chants is wrong, it was more monkey noises and comments from the crowd. There's no doubt about it, there was a lot of that, not as bad as some places, but it was bad enough. It was around the time when a lot more black players started to come in. It was ugly, and there'd be all these stereotypes about how black players didn't have any bottle.'

Chris has also seen a new generation of Spurs fans adopt the label of 'yids'. For many fans, using the term is about reclaiming what was an insult hurled by other fans, but it's something which divides the Spurs support.

'I feel very uncomfortable with this "yids" thing,' says Chris. 'My parents were in the Battle of Cable Street. I'm old enough to remember the fascists in Ridley Road, and that would've been what they shouted, "We've gotta get rid of the yids." So even accepting that the later generation doesn't know anything about it and isn't doing it for those reasons at all, it still sends a shiver down my spine when I hear it. So I can't possibly shout it, and I don't really like other people shouting it either.

'The whole Jewish thing at Spurs never really meant that much to me – Spurs was a tribal loyalty rather than anything to do with religion.'

In recent years Spurs have waned as a power in the game, and Chris reckons a major turning point was 'when all that PLC business started, things taking over that weren't to do with football, all the merchandising . . . You'd be mugs not to use the possibilities, but not make that the major thing.

'When Scholar and co. turned up and started talking about being a PLC, it didn't frighten me, but I didn't like it especially. Over time it just became clear that things weren't what they should be. The pronouncements coming from Scholar and the board were a bit worrying – you never heard anything from the board when they were winning Doubles and so on.'

One encounter with the old board that Chris remembers illustrates that the more things change, the more things really do stay the same. 'I met Sid Wale once, the chairman of the Spurs. I was in the press box, right towards the end of Nicholson's time, sitting next to Danny Blanchflower, my all-time hero. I'd pinched somebody's press card to watch it and I said to Danny, because they were playing really badly, I said, "How can you watch this?" And he said, "Ah, the game behind the game." What I didn't realise was that he was there to talk about getting the job. Nicholson wanted him to get it, but they chickened out of it. Then I spoke to Wale, the son, a real chinless wonder, and I said, "You know people are interested in Danny Blanchflower being the manager," and he said [posh voice], "No comment – but don't quote me." Ha, ha, ha! I thought, there's a cautious man.'

There has been real change, though, not least the emergence of organised fans' groups. Chris, perhaps not surprisingly, sees this as a positive development. 'The [Supporters'] Trust that's going on now, I think that's a great innovation, the idea that you can actually talk to the people in charge.

'I've seen a lot of that fan groups and publications stuff as part of the explosion of literature and hot air around the game, but a lot of it is very well informed and is thinking about things that didn't used to be thought about. There should be proper representation for the fans, but the difficulty is getting the representative view. The big challenge is to find a way of getting the essence of those views out and having the machinery to influence the people that make the decisions. So many of these pronouncements are completely divorced from reality.'

Chris thinks that the 'fickle' tag, which so infuriates many Spurs fans, does have some resonance.

'I think the crowd are quite fickle,' he says. 'When I first took the children, Gary Lineker was playing for Spurs. Marvellous player. He scored a goal, and then he missed a couple and a few people behind us were bad-mouthing him to such a degree that it was impossible to explain to my children how that would happen, people that would come just to criticise. I tend to see the positive side of most things, sometimes that means I bend over too far to make excuses for 'em.

But I think there is a peculiar bunch of fans here that almost wants to turn on the team before they've done something wrong, but also appreciates good football as well.

'My son blames me now for inflicting all this misery on him. Every year it gets worse. He's become like a modern fan, in that he's quick to criticise, whereas we're the seen-it-all-before character, we like to see the optimistic side.'

So what are Chris's own views on two of the most influential and controversial names of recent years? On Glenn Hoddle's managerial tenure he is forthright but genuinely perplexed.

'I thought he'd do the job when he came, even though I thought he was a nutcase. I was pleased when he came, that was partly the complete idolatry of him as a player, but then he'd shown himself to be a complete lunatic not just by the things he'd said but also by the things he was doing, like writing the book about being England manager, which *must* turn everybody against you. I'd met him as well, and I was just surprised that he ever went into management, let alone be a successful manager.'

And what about Sol Campbell? Chris is again forthright.

'It was like one of your own turning against you. I could well understand his frustration about being in a team that wasn't getting anywhere, but then to leave it so Spurs didn't get any money after stringing 'em along, and two, to join the hated rivals – our captain. My bile for him is pretty fundamental. Well, I don't know if you can have fundamental bile, but I truly want bad things for him. It's partly a football fan speaking, but partly that I find his behaviour unforgivable.'

That opinion would appear to rule Campbell out of Chris's list of favourites. So who would be on it?

'Danny Blanchflower is obviously one, Dave Mackay, Glenn Hoddle, Jürgen Klinsmann, Tommy Harmer the Charmer . . .' muses Chris. 'I think I'd make Harmer my favourite, because he was a tiny little character, but he just seemed to float above the mud. When I later took Tommy to a game, he was amazed at how light the balls were. I once saw him bounce the ball against the corner flag to get past someone. He had that skill, and somehow that was just Spurs, a kind of home-made, Hackney Marshes skill. He was from Edmonton.

'He'd be the favourite, and the best is a toss-up between Danny

Blanchflower and Dave Mackay. Danny Blanchflower if you can incorporate his captaincy into it, because he could change a game. It's not pure football skill, it's using your head. You don't have to have people standing on the touch-line waving their arms about. That's why he got in trouble with the manager: he stuck the centre-half up front and they stuck him in the reserves for a couple of games.

'But Dave Mackay for skill and heart, and never knowing when he was beaten. I was at the game when he broke his leg against Manchester United in the European Cup. It was a bad tackle by Noel Cantwell, and when he was coming back he broke his leg again in the reserves. But he came back again. Eric Butler, who was one of the Wapping refuseniks who worked for us at the T&G for a while, he used to ghost a column for Dave Mackay, and the day after he broke his leg the first time he arrives round at Eric's driving a car, with the leg in plaster. Whether Eric used a bit of hyperbole I don't know, but that did fit in with the bloke. Since then I have met him and he's full of humility, he's not a big "I am".

'Tommy Harmer I've since met at the Footballer of the Year dinner and a couple of other things, and he says how other players looked up to Danny Blanchflower. Tactically he was a genius, but he also knew the politics of the organisation, so if people wanted things done they would do it through Danny because he knew how it all worked. If ever you wanted someone to sum up the Spurs it was Danny Blanchflower. He was an independent sort of a character, he played beautiful football, but also he had his head screwed on and he was able to change things as the game went on. Which, of course, was what put him in opposition to the kind of control freaks that even then was running the club.'

If Chris Kaufman was destined to support Spurs by dint of the time and place he was born in, Jeremy Dear arrived by a very different route. 'I've never been one who's lived within a stone's throw of White Hart Lane and been able to get there easily,' he says. 'I was living in Leatherhead at the time I first saw Spurs, I think it was probably about 1971, and I spent most of my youth growing up abroad in the end, in Belgium.'

In fact, a lifetime's dedication to Spurs came about quite by accident. 'I think I was meant to be a Chelsea fan actually,' Jeremy laughs. 'My mum used to work night shifts as a nurse, so my dad had to take us out of the house on a Saturday so she could go to sleep. We got bored of going to Chessington Zoo and places like that every weekend, so one of my dad's friends took us to a football match. I was one of those kids who loved running around chasing a football, so I was really excited. He took me to Chelsea–Tottenham, and Tottenham won, so, like kids of that age, I decided to support Tottenham. That was when Pat Jennings was in goal and he saved a penalty that day.

'I always wanted to be a goalkeeper, a professional goalkeeper, so Pat Jennings was my hero. We had some League Cup victories around that time as well, so that consolidated my support for them. At that time virtually all my schoolmates were Liverpool fans, 'cos Liverpool were just going into their really successful years, and I always like to be different, so choosing Tottenham was one of the things in my rebellious streak,' he laughs.

'I would listen to commentary on the radio a lot. I remember things like the season we were promoted back from the old Second Division when we drew on the final day of the season, 0–0 at Southampton, and we had to get at least a point and it was a real nail-biter. I was in the back of the car, we were going to see my granddad in Portsmouth and I was twisting the radio in every direction to keep the signal.

'I was about eight or nine at the time we're talking about, and travelling from Surrey up to north London on my own wasn't something I would have done. When I was ten, I moved abroad, so it wasn't really a possibility.'

Moving abroad would have nipped most teenagers' growing obsession in the bud, but Jeremy sees it as something of a lucky break.

'I saw the very first match Ossie Ardiles and Ricky Villa played for Tottenham because it was a friendly at Antwerp in Belgium,' he remembers. 'We won 3–1 in a cold, empty Antwerp stadium. That night, in fact, Ricky Villa looked like a world-beater and Ossie Ardiles looked like he'd never be able to cope with European football, yet it turned out so differently.

'And I got to see the UEFA Cup final against Anderlecht at Anderlecht.'

By this time, English fans had already developed a reputation for hooliganism in Europe, and with Tottenham supporters having been particularly involved in the Low Countries, Jeremy had an unusual perspective. He's honest enough to admit that, as a teenager, he also had a different view.

'I do remember being conscious of crowd trouble. There was a slight edge, which I quite liked, 'cos I don't think I ever actually saw the worst of any real violence, but as a kid I quite liked that edginess. That's certainly not there any more.

'Going to see football matches was more exciting then. I don't know if it was more exciting that I seemed to be a young kid in an adult world. There were also some really bad times for football. While I was living in Belgium I was at the Arsenal–Valencia Cup-Winners' Cup final that was at the Heysel stadium and there was tremendous trouble, and there was a Villa–Anderlecht match there where one of my mates was hit by riot police as they waded into the crowd behind the goal. There were some pretty nasty nights, and I'd hate to glorify any of the stupid hooliganism and tribalism that went on, but there was a certain excitement about the terraces, about being packed in, the chanting, the singing . . .'

One of the verses to the Spurs version of 'Glory, Glory Hallelujah' contains the line 'We're loyal Spurs supporters and we come to every game', but Jeremy is another of the many fans who, despite circumstances preventing them from doing that, are no less loyal.

'In Belgium, I was a Tottenham fan in exile, that's the phrase I used to use. I love going to see live football, but nothing beats going to see Tottenham. I'd still rather watch Hull City v. Tottenham on a sodden pitch on a Tuesday night than Real Madrid play Man United in the Champions League final, because there's a passion in one and just an interest in the other.

'Now, I have a job that unfortunately means I work an awful lot of Saturdays and I'm away at conferences, but I have my mobile phone that vibrates every time there's a goal at Tottenham, so even if I'm in the middle of a speech at a rostrum I can still check the score.

'I haven't got a season ticket because I work so many Saturdays. For the first time in my life I can afford a season ticket, but I don't have the time to do it because of my job. However, there are a number of union officials from all different unions who all support Tottenham, and a number of them have season tickets so, because of the nature of all our jobs there is always someone who can't make it and therefore the season tickets get offered round. So I do get along a few times a season.'

Jeremy has an interesting take on the reputation of Spurs fans.

'Probably the reputation of Tottenham fans is worst in Holland. I went to a Feyenoord match when a home-made bomb was found on a train that was meant to take Tottenham fans to the game. But I've travelled lots round the world. I was in Ethiopia in January, and I had my Tottenham shirt on, on top of a mountain village in Ethiopia, and someone – it was just after Robbie Keane had scored his first hat-trick for Tottenham – someone leaned out the window of a bus that was passing and shouted, "Keano, Keano." Some young Ethiopian kid! Wherever I've gone and I've worn the shirt, I've always found a relatively good response.'

Spurs fans also have a reputation for organising and campaigning, so it's interesting to hear how a trade-union general secretary views this.

'At times I've been to meetings of probably all the fan groups, as a political activist, to try and help out,' says Jeremy, warming to the theme. 'I'm a real believer that fans should have a say in the running of their football club, and at one or two clubs there's been some quite interesting developments, the supporters' trusts and things like that. I would certainly love to see Tottenham fans have more of a say, and anything I individually could do to help I would be happy to do.

'I see plenty of politics at Tottenham, but it's normally in the pub beforehand, given the group of people I go to football with. You have David Triesman, the General Secretary of the Labour Party, Charlie Whelan – it's a kind of bizarre mixture of the left of British society, from the soft to the hard left. Some of us go into the cheap seats and some of us go into the executive boxes, ha ha!

'In some ways football still is one of those areas where there could be much more radical movements of supporters, and supporters could get together and use their clout a lot more than they do. When you think these clubs totally rely on the finance of these supporters, supporters' organisations should consequently have much more say in the running of the club. But they are very deliberately kept out by those people who realise that supporters will on the whole make the prices cheaper and the facilities better and things like that, which goes against the ethos of the shareholders and businesses that own the clubs. It's profit at any expense.

'There is a role on the board for supporter representatives, for community representatives – you look at that area around White Hart Lane, it's a pretty impoverished area of London with lots and lots of social problems, and you've got this gleaming stadium with all the fancy cars of the players parked in the private car park, and you've got the boarded-up shops . . . That's an issue. Here is a vastly wealthy football club in the middle of a community in London that has lots of problems. Some of the facilities at Tottenham can be available to the local community, and there are cooperative forms of ownership where the supporters and community could have much more clout. Now people will probably say that's pie in the sky, it might be all right for a Third Division club . . . But I don't accept that, I think you could get the fans and the community on board with a model that gave something back.'

What happens to White Hart Lane is becoming a bigger issue, despite the board's obfuscation, and Jeremy has some strong views here too.

'No sharing with Arsenal. I differ from Charlie Whelan on this one,' he says with feeling. 'I would be loath for Tottenham to move out of that area. The ideal situation would be for the council to grant permission to expand the ground. Whether that depends on transport links – and to be honest, transport links are rubbish – they need to sort that out, but I would hate them to move out of London or to east London. They're still a club that draws a lot of support from the local area.

'In King's Cross, where the NUJ is based, we're probably right on the edge of that area. Round here there's a division between Arsenal and Tottenham fans – one pub will be Arsenal and one will be Tottenham. It would be wrong to lose that.'

Although Jeremy could, and would, debate the wider social issues all night, he's just as opinionated on the more basic issue of favourite players.

'When I played football, I was kind of a harsh centre-back – some of the people I played against might call me dirty, but I'll say harsh or tough – so there were people like Graham Roberts and Steve Perryman who weren't the greatest footballers on earth, but they gave everything for Tottenham and I loved that about them. But for just the sheer joy of watching, I'd probably have to go with Glenn Hoddle, and it pains me to say it after the experience of the last couple of years – and it's a lesson to everyone who was the king at a football club not to go back and try and manage them – but he was fantastic.

'One of the things I loved was when we had Crooks and Archibald up front – they scored so many goals. Now we struggle to find anyone to score 15 in a season, but that year they were knocking 'em in all over the place, about 40-odd goals. It was exciting and good to watch.

'Ginola on his day was fantastic, but he had too many patchy performances as well; Klinsmann came back and did a great job, Sheringham too did some great things, but if I had one choice it would be Jennings – my hero, because I grew up with him.'

Typically Tottenham, Jeremy's best and worst moments come in the FA Cup.

'I can think of a few best moments . . . um . . . probably the ultimate cliché, but the Ricky Villa goal in the Cup final against Man City. I wasn't there, but we'd been so disappointing in the first match, and his dream appeared to have died and everything had gone wrong, and for that to happen was a fantastic night.

'The one I remember for sheer excitement was winning the UEFA Cup, the Anderlecht game, because I saw both legs, I was there. The penalty shoot-out, Tony Parks, the third-choice keeper, saving the final penalty – it was just a classic.

'The worst was when I was a student in Coventry the year we lost the Cup final, and there were two Tottenham fans in the whole of Coventry. One was the breakfast show presenter on the radio, and the other one was me. On the day they paraded the FA Cup through the streets, I think I was [laughs] the loneliest man on earth, the only person in the whole of Coventry not out on the streets celebrating.'

So what's next for Spurs?

'The thing I want to see, that I haven't seen for a number of years, is passion and absolute determination to try and win whatever the circumstances,' says Jeremy. 'A lot of my favourite players are those that play with a passion rather than being the most beautiful player or most skilful passer, someone who has that will to win.

'You ask any fan at any club and they'll say they love the people that play their heart out for the shirt. It's all so commercial now – players transfer so quickly – that that kind of real heart-in-the-club person is valued.'

10

To see Tottenham win away: Paul Taylor

> Jingle bells, jingle bells
> Jingle all the way
> Oh what fun it is to see
> Tottenham win away

As the close of the January 2004 transfer window approached, speculation spiralled as the names of alleged transfer targets emerged. Players that Spurs were interested in, like Nottingham Forest's Andy Reid and Michael Dawson, were overwhelmingly young and England-based. Trapattoni, it was argued, was unlikely to know them, so the new manager must be Sven. Or Martin O'Neill. Or, well, insert your own rumour here.

What was obvious was that Spurs needed to make some signings, and the club did get off the blocks quickly by securing midfielder Michael Brown from Sheffield United. The price of £500,000 looked like a steal for one of the First Division's most highly regarded players, but he wasn't the dominant figure Spurs so clearly needed. Did the club have the financial clout to net any targets?

For Paul Taylor this, rather than glory, glory nights or famous cup victories, had been the defining characteristic of his support for Spurs. A 20-year-old student, he saw his first game a year after Spurs last won the FA Cup in 1991. His take on Spurs is not only shaped by this event, but by the fact that he was born and bred in the north.

'I'm a Yorkshire lad through and through,' says Paul, in an accent a million miles away from the nasal twang of N17. To the ears of a Londoner, it sounds strange: northern fans, runs the cliché, support their home-town club; at a push they may follow Manchester United or Liverpool. But Spurs? Why on earth would a young lad barely out of his teens from 200 miles away up in Leeds want to support Spurs?

'I don't think I've got any attachment to north London really because my roots are up here, but I do have strong feelings for Tottenham the club,' he says. 'I identify with White Hart Lane because it's Spurs' home. Obviously, whether Spurs play in Tottenham or not doesn't really affect me (travelling-wise) but I personally think Tottenham should play in Tottenham and at White Hart Lane. I didn't actually go there until 1995, but when I did it was a fabulous experience; I felt at home.'

Paul's devotion to Tottenham is an illustration that, at a time when it is assumed every young fan simply follows the most successful team, not everyone is a lazy glory-hunter. His introduction to the world of fandom came at an all-too brief period in modern times when Spurs gave a passable impression of a successful club, but subsequent years would have tested even the most masochistic of fans. Despite that, Paul has stayed defiantly faithful to the cause.

If the theory that a club chooses its fans and not vice versa is true, then Paul is living proof that clubs can still attract followers for all kinds of strange reasons other than by dangling glittering prizes in front of their eyes. Location did not play a part and neither did family association in Paul's recruitment to the Tottenham fold. Instead, Spurs caught the imagination of Paul Taylor by way of television and one of the nation's most famous footballing near-misses.

'I was interested in football from a very early age, but my dad didn't influence me because he's mainly into rugby league and running. I can't put an exact date on when I first started supporting Spurs, but I reckon I was seven or eight, meaning it was sometime in 1990 or 1991.

'My real interest really kicked off during Italia '90. The whole tournament was on TV and all the emotion and the drama caught my imagination, I suppose, and I was addicted from then on. Gary Lineker and Paul Gascoigne helped get England to the semi-finals and I think it was these two who sparked my passion for Tottenham, so my first memory of actually "supporting" Spurs in a major game was the '91 FA Cup final against Nottingham Forest.'

Such initial excitement no doubt played a part in the then

impressionable eight-year-old's conversion to the Tottenham cause, but it is not as if he didn't have greater temptations closer at hand. The Leeds United of the early 1990s were a leading outfit and Howard Wilkinson's team lifted the League title in 1992. Unlike the majority of his school friends, however, Paul's loyalty lay with a club from outside his own city. And yet, he wasn't a lone voice in what many would assume to be a Tottenham-free wilderness.

'Throughout my time at school there have always been several other Spurs fans in my year right up until I did my A levels, so I wasn't all on my own.'

Neither, perhaps more surprisingly, did Paul and his fellow Spurs-supporting schoolmates have to suffer any extra mickey-taking or hostility from fans who followed local clubs.

'I wouldn't say I received any extra "stick" from mates because I support Spurs. Like any other kid at school who likes football, you are bound to get some stick when you lose and the banter that goes with supporting a different team.

'It's amazing, actually, because despite our lack of success there are quite a few Spurs fans "oop north". More often than not when I'm out shopping I'll see someone in a Spurs shirt. Fortunately the same can't be said about Arsenal and Chelsea, but I'm sure they're getting much more popular with the younger kids.'

How long Tottenham will still be able to seduce a new generation of fans in or outside of the club's immediate catchment area remains to be seen, but now that Paul has been well and truly hooked, he is as passionate and committed as any fan from London.

Football fundamentalists may object and there are certainly some southerners who resent supporters whom they perceive as 'outsiders'. Indeed, as would be clear to anyone who has travelled to games up the M1 and M6 in the last 30 years, regionalist contempt for 'northerners' is a prejudice that runs deep among many fans, whichever of the capital's clubs they follow. However, if Paul has been subject to a lack of hospitality, it hasn't put him off.

'Some fans can be indifferent when they hear my accent or on the Internet message boards when some people have a bit of an attitude if they find out where I'm from, but I would say 95 per cent of Spurs fans have been great and really friendly. I would never say I've been treated in a hostile manner, because, at the end of the day, we are all following the same team.'

'Following' for Paul isn't easy. As a schoolboy he ran his own very popular website 'spursonline', which enabled him to communicate with his fellow fans. Now at university, he can still chew the Spurs fat, but the chances of seeing his team in the flesh are more limited.

'I mainly go to away games in the north and the Midlands. When I was younger, it was hard to keep up to date with happenings at Spurs, with only Ceefax and snippets in the northern editions of the papers during the week and *Match of the Day*, but with Sky Sports, the Internet and all the other sources it's much easier to keep in touch.

'The most difficult part of supporting Spurs is obviously the distance. To go to a home game will take up a full day, which I don't mind, but it can be quite expensive for a student once I've bought the ticket, train ticket, food and drink, etc.'

Because of the costs and distances involved it is a common occurrence for Tottenham 'exiles' to get their first experience of seeing Spurs in the flesh at their local ground. Any supporter of any club large or small will confirm that following your team on the road is a totally different experience to that at home: the atmosphere is often more threatening, the sense of camaraderie, loyalty and togetherness among your fellow fans that much stronger. Such has been Tottenham's miserable away record in recent seasons that a sense of doom might be another shared emotion, but for the eight-year-old Paul his first exposure to the 'Tottenham Experience' made a lasting impression.

'The first game I went to was in 1992, I think, at Elland Road, Leeds. I went with a neighbour and sat with the Leeds fans. I remember going to the game quite clearly. The final score was 1–1 and we went ahead, if memory serves me right, with David Howells's header, but to be honest it could have been another player. That kind of thing didn't stick in the memory so much as the experience – the noise, the excitement, seeing and hearing Spurs fans singing songs about *my* club. It was an enjoyable day and obviously it didn't put me off supporting Tottenham because here I am now, over ten years later and they are still my club.

'The main reason I started to support Spurs was due to Gary Lineker (his goal-scoring exploits and general attitude to the game were what appealed) and Gazza; he'd left Spurs by then, but he was still associated with the club. I thought he was daft and still do, but the fact that Spurs were a club who could have a superstar like him was important – something that said Spurs were a big draw.'

Superstars have been thin on the ground at Tottenham in the last decade, especially those of the English variety. Paul Gascoigne was a bona-fide legend – a talent not realised to the full, perhaps, but a player who could command headlines for Tottenham.

Gascoigne's departure, however, marked yet another of those watersheds in Tottenham's recent history of decline. He was sold to balance the books – a case of cold financial reality after the free-spending chutzpah and mismanagement of the Irving Scholar years and an admittance that Spurs could not compete with the big boys any more. As Tottenham proved season after season through the 1990s, spending big money was not a problem; attracting genuine talent was.

It was Paul's misfortune to become a Spurs supporter just as this harsh new reality dawned. 'When I first started supporting, we were still regarded as a big, big club, but we were just saved from bankruptcy. I was too young, though, to know all the ins and outs of what happened financially. Since then it's been a frustrating story of the same thing, really. It's been one "transitional" season after another, it's been quite depressing; I think I'm the jinx.

'The worst time was probably around the time we were facing relegation. I forget which season it was, but we played a "must win" game away at Oldham, which we won 2–0. The Gross period was a nightmare too, also whenever Stuart Nethercott was playing in our central defence! Those were bad times.'

Such bad times have been lifted only occasionally by glimmers of excitement redolent of a more impressive Tottenham past. Two stand out for Paul: first, the one-season wonder of Jürgen Klinsmann's mid-1990s English sojourn and, second, the false dawn of the victorious League Cup campaign of 1999 inspired by David Ginola, another flair player out of place among the general dross.

Klinsmann dug Spurs out of a tricky hole at the time. Similarly, Ginola had temporarily saved George Graham's managerial bacon, but, in a *dénouement* that typified the gradual betrayal of Tottenham's traditions, the Frenchman was subsequently rewarded with contemptuous treatment by Graham and eventually sold.

So instead of seeing an array of players cast in the Tottenham mould, Paul has had to make do with common or garden pros; instead of players of the calibre of Jimmy Greaves, Ossie Ardiles and

Glenn Hoddle, he has had to suffer the likes of more 'industrious' talents such as Kevin Scott, Ramon Vega and Ben Thatcher – hardly the stuff of the glory, glory game.

'We've had plenty of poor players in my time,' says Paul, 'but it's always more disappointing when a player signs with a fantastic reputation and totally flops in our colours. I had high hopes for Nicola Berti, but he never performed, but I would have to say the biggest disappointment was Sergei Rebrov.

'I remember all the hype when he signed – "He's the player who made Shevchenko tick", etc. I also remember downloading some of his goals when I was in my free periods at college and showing them off to my mates. It all looked so good, but I would have to say he is the most disappointing player of all, a great waste.'

Any mention of Rebrov to a Spurs fan will probably result in the same look of horror that appears on the face of an Old Labour stalwart when the issue of the Millennium Dome is raised in polite company – a painful reminder of how to waste valuable money fast. For whatever reason, Tottenham's £11 million record signing was not a success at White Hart Lane, his fate a glaring demonstration of Tottenham's newly found status as also-rans.

Tottenham fans have been chastened by the Rebrov debacle – an example of how Spurs had lost 'the Spurs Way'. For many younger fans, however, who haven't had the pleasure of seeing their side perform in such a manner, this ethos hangs like a millstone around the club's neck. Paul is certainly one of those who would swap pretty football for winning football, yet he still believes in the club's traditional reputation.

'It's a tricky one. I've always heard about the so-called "Spurs Way"; unfortunately I have seen no evidence of it except some games under Ossie [Ardiles], so it's hard to say I believe in it. I would love to see this Spurs Way, though! I suppose I'm too young. Having said that, we should be proud of our history, but our history does not give us a divine right to win things now or in the future.'

Probably for that reason, the highlights of Paul's life as a Spurs fan concern events rather than performances. 'It was a disappointing result but the 2001 FA Cup semi-final at Old Trafford was my most memorable game. My first "north London derby", Glenn Hoddle's first game in charge and Campbell's last game in our colours. A brilliant atmosphere, especially when [Gary] Doherty scored out of the blue, but the final score was a gutter. Another couple of games which I will always remember are the 4–3 victory at Sheffield Wednesday [Jürgen Klinsmann's debut game] and the 6–2 win in the Cup against Southampton.'

Some might argue the latter was remarkable not because of four goals from the legendary though limited Ronnie Rosenthal but only in that Spurs came back from 2–0 down at half-time to beat a side they would have been expected to defeat with some ease in the 'good old days'. In the not-so-good present Paul is part of a support at odds with itself: one respectful of the standards its club has to live up to, but keenly aware that even moderate progress is all that Spurs can realistically hope for.

How even that reduced ambition can be achieved is subject to any number of theories. As a member of Save Our Spurs (SOS), the pressure group formed with the express aim of ousting Alan Sugar, stage one for Paul has been achieved. He admits, however, that 'SOS served its purpose and achieved what the "majority" of the fans wanted. Looking back, though, are we any better off with Enic in charge instead of Sugar? To be honest, I haven't seen much difference, but only time will tell.

'As usual there seems to be a lot of politics and hidden agendas in the boardroom at the moment. I was unsure of Enic's motives when they first took control because after all they are an investment company wishing to make money, but because the football bubble has burst I'm unsure what's going to happen. I think one of the best options would be to take Tottenham private (whether that's Levy or somebody else) because Stock Exchange regulations seem to be limiting us at the moment. I also don't think we need a Director of Football; that's not [David] Pleat's fault but it causes too many problems.'

And what of the current team – a side which, when Paul was speaking, had suffered seven defeats in just fourteen League games of the 2003–04 season and was reckoned by some older supporters to be one of the worst in Tottenham's post-war history? Paul had this to say: 'Individually we have some very good players and quite a few international players, and if they click under the right manager using the right system we could do reasonably well. Individually at the back we have very good defenders, but they are prone to errors.

'If they cut out these errors and defend properly as a unit, things should improve. Maybe one reason for our poor defensive record is due to our very poor midfield. The midfield really worries me, and whoever is appointed full time will have to sort out the midfield as his first job. It lacks spark, pace, bite and needs a complete overhaul.'

Part of that overhaul process came with the removal of Glenn Hoddle. Unlike the romantic nostalgists, whose memory of Hoddle the player prevented them from seeing the shortcomings of Hoddle the manager, Paul is honest in his assessment of the fallen hero: 'I never had the pleasure of seeing Hoddle play in a Tottenham shirt so his playing days never clouded my judgement. It's all very disappointing because there were massive expectations when he took over, but, to be brutally honest, he simply didn't achieve the desired results.

'Our League record was appalling from January 2003 onwards and we got knocked out of both cup competitions early on which lost us vital revenue. I also think it was obvious the players lost confidence in the manager. I personally think he should have gone in the summer, but fair play to the board for giving him the cash to try and improve things. It was obvious early on in the season nothing had improved, so it was time for him to go. Unfortunately it's another season wasted.'

In other words, yet another season of transition. Paul Taylor may not have been a Tottenham fan for long, but he is clearly learning what it means to be a follower of a club languishing in the doldrums.

11

My eyes have seen the glory:
Aubrey Morris

My eyes have seen the glory of the cups at White Hart Lane
And the Spurs go marching on
Glory, Glory Hallelujah . . .

On the last day of January, Spurs went to Loftus Road and lost for the first time in 2004 to Fulham, despite going 1–0 up courtesy of a Robbie Keane penalty. On Monday, 2 February, the transfer window would close and Spurs looked to have missed the boat again. As that Monday unfolded, only the Paul Robinson deal seemed on, and bizarrely Spurs were proposing that he stay 'on loan' at Leeds until the end of the season.

Then, two hours before the deadline, came major news, unbelievable news. Jermain Defoe was to sign for Spurs.

Defoe was the hottest young striking property in English football. It was taken as read that such a proven goal-scorer would go to one of the big three, yet Spurs had got him – Spurs who were no longer the moneybags club, Spurs who were being painted as perennial underachievers. It was a good day to be a Spurs fan, but as usual there were ominous signs to cloud the silver lining.

The Robinson deal had fallen through because it contravened Premier League rules on loan deals between clubs – was this another example of Daniel Levy trying to be too clever by half? Despite the embarrassment of riches up front, there was still no defensive midfielder. And while the Defoe signing was widely applauded, David Pleat let slip that the club had only decided to go in for him after the Fulham defeat, a game in which Spurs created the most chances but failed to capitalise on them. Was this an inspired move, or more panic?

It was all a long way from the 'Glory Days' of the early 1960s, days which loom large over anyone who has played for or supported Tottenham Hotspur since then, in equal measure a source of pride and a burden. They were extraordinary times to be a Spurs fan, and it's fitting that such times produced an extraordinary supporter.

Aubrey Morris's life had already been eventful enough by the time Bill Nicholson's team embarked on their journey into immortality. Born in 1919 in Bethnal Green into a family of Jewish bakers, he'd fought Mosley's fascist blackshirts on Cable Street, organised support for Republican Spain and been evacuated from Dunkirk. And now he was about to take the simple practice of supporting a football team to new heights – literally.

'I organised the first air travel for football supporters,' says Aubrey. 'I did it with a man called Sid Silver who was in the travel business with me, who was also a Spurs supporter, for the Spurs game against Sunderland when they drew 1–1 up there in the FA Cup, that would have been 1961. We came down here and won 5–0. That was the first-ever air charter for football supporters.'

Nowadays, the idea of travelling to watch your team abroad is seen almost as a rite of passage, with the passport as familiar a prop to fans of successful teams today as a rattle and muffler were years ago. But in 1961–62 the whole concept of following your team in Europe was new. This was a time before mass-market package travel had made the Costa del Sol as familiar a holiday spot as Southend or Brighton had been before, and European competition had long been looked upon with disdain by the insular English authorities. So when Spurs won the Double they became only the fourth English team, after Manchester United, Wolves and Burnley, to compete with all the champions of Europe for the European Cup. The Cup itself had only ever been won by two teams, Real Madrid (five times) and Benfica (twice), so there was great excitement at the prospect of Bill Nicholson's Super Spurs making their mark.

English teams had little experience in Europe, and for supporters following the side abroad it really was a leap into the unknown, but Aubrey Morris was the right man in the right place at the right time, and it was his vision, organisation and determination that ushered in the modern era of football support.

It all started with that first trip to the north-east of England, and Aubrey remembers it well. 'I became a taxi driver and I got involved in the travel business organising charter holidays for taxi drivers in about 1956,' he says. 'I was going to Spurs more regularly. I was living in Stamford Hill at the time, and got to know people. All the away trips were in the UK and they used to have coach trips, but I didn't really bother with them because I didn't have the time – it used to take all day. Because I was setting up my holiday company at the time, I wondered if it would be possible that people might be interested in going by air.'

It was a bold idea, but would people go for it? And, more immediately, how would they hear about such an opportunity?

'We issued leaflets,' says Aubrey. 'My family stood outside the ground after and before the game.'

As interest grew, Aubrey approached the club, but, true to form, the club was wary of a new idea. 'I was introduced to Hymie Lewis and John Edwards, the treasurer and secretary of the Spurs Supporters' Club, by Sid Silver and they said, "It's a good idea, but we can't take on a responsibility like that," he remembers. 'So I took the responsibility on myself. I did this deal and 47 of us, including my son and myself, went.

'We flew into Newcastle via Gatwick, and then by coach to Sunderland and the ground. I had a plane, a Viscount from Maitland Drewery Aviation, that seated 84 and I had 47 on it. So, I did a deal with the company and they agreed: "Give us the cash, whatever you've got, and we'll go." This was all as I was starting up in the tour-operating business.

'It was all right, except the tickets we had were in the Sunderland supporters' section. It was a very ferocious game. Blanchflower had to calm his own players down. It was like a madhouse. We daren't even speak; we daren't even let them know we weren't from that part of the world. When they equalised, there was a pitch invasion and we genuinely feared for our lives.

'But we came away from there and we'd all bonded together, we'd experienced something. When we got back to Gatwick, the plane was impounded, we'd just about managed to get it in.'

Those 47 supporters had started something, but still the club kept its distance officially. It didn't put Aubrey off.

'We got into going to all the other games, going abroad. [There was] probably a nucleus of about 100 who came to every one of the games. We kept putting leaflets out at every home game. The club knew we were doing it, but they didn't want any part of it.

'If we went on a trip and we stayed overnight we stayed in the same hotel as the players, and we saw what they were like. I had long chats with Danny Blanchflower, which was interesting. The supporters mixed in.

'It grew from there, until when we got to the Cup-Winners' Cup final in 1963 against Atletico Madrid it became a very big operation. I got 33 aircraft to fly from Southend and Gatwick to Rotterdam airport. The telephones were ringing and I got friends and relatives on the phones taking calls. It was like a little hothouse there in the office we had in Bishopsgate, almost opposite Liverpool Street station. We carried 2,500. I was getting aircraft from all over, all different sizes, all different sorts, Argonauts, Elizabethans, Dakotas, DC3s . . . In those days it was different to now. After the war you had an Air Force pilot, and if he got himself a DC3 he became an airline, and they'd have to get what business they could. So people were queuing up outside the office and I got 33 aircraft and that was it, I'd used up all the capacity.'

You'd think that only the relatively well-off could afford the time and money to travel in those days, but Aubrey says that wasn't so.

'We had kids queuing up, youngsters, with the money, eight pounds ten shillings. It was a day trip to Rotterdam, so it wasn't all that much time, and eight pounds was quite a bit of money, but it was reasonable, people could accept it. We had a real mix of people. The first flight was mainly people who had money, the Sunderland one, because they could have gone by coach, but it was the sort of thing people with money would do. But I gave a couple of people a lift in my car to Gatwick on the morning of the Rotterdam game and they were just ordinary people, a retired tailor, that sort of thing, but old-time Spurs supporters.

'Rotterdam was quite incredible. My regret is I never took any photographs, because I never thought anything of it.'

That Rotterdam trip to see Tottenham Hotspur become the first British team to win a European trophy was the culmination of a project that had grown and grown over two seasons for Aubrey and his company, Riviera Holidays.

'In Rotterdam we had 60 coaches lined up with the name of my company on them,' says Aubrey. 'My son Michael and I missed the last goal because we had to go out and see that everything was all right for people, but seeing those coaches was very exciting indeed. It was very much a leap into the unknown. We did all the European games.'

The pressure must have been enormous, but there were benefits.

'In the 1962 European Cup run, we drew Benfica, who were at their peak at the time, and that meant a trip to Lisbon,' remembers Aubrey. 'We put together a one-day trip, a two-night trip with hotel accommodation and three- and five-night trips travelling by ferry from Southampton to Lisbon and return. It was our greatest challenge, and we had to go over in advance to check everything. We took the opportunity to explore. It was gorgeous weather. You could sit down to eat at ten or eleven in the evening, and I remember it was the first time I could choose live fish, including lobster, from a tank in the middle of the room.

'Kick-off would have been about ten at night, and that was glorious; nobody had ever experienced that. Warm weather at ten o'clock.'

Passengers had to be organised just as much as every other detail.

'We had to really nurture people,' says Aubrey. 'The majority of them never had a passport. We did packages, took care of people from when they got on the plane to when they got off back home.

'We'd book hotels and everything else. One guy, he left his wallet in a cab, and he didn't speak any Portuguese, so I said, "Don't worry, I'll get you sorted out," and he never left me. I'd go to the toilet and he'd be there. Ha, ha! But it was that kind of bonding, that closeness. Once they got overseas, we looked after them entirely.'

That service provided Aubrey with some testing times.

'On one of the games we went to Czechoslovakia,' he says. 'We were playing Dukla Prague, who were the Czech champions, and when you went to Eastern Europe in those days you had to buy currency when you got in there and you weren't allowed to take it away with you. They promised me they'd have somebody at the airport on the way back. They didn't, and the pilot wouldn't wait, he said it'd cost £100 an hour to wait. Well, we just couldn't afford that, it would have been the end of us. So I got everyone's money together and made a list. I had 200 people with me, we got back, and I went to the Czech embassy and harangued them and eventually we got the money back.'

Despite the official supporters' club and the club itself keeping their distance, the players and management acknowledged the efforts of the travelling support.

'I went to see Nicholson on two or three occasions, and he was very pleased we had all the supporters there,' says Aubrey. 'The supporters' club would never have undertaken that sort of risk. But Nicholson appreciated it, and Danny Blanchflower appreciated it. The trouble with being with the players was that, well, they talk about what football players are like now, but they weren't much different then, but with less money.'

However, it was the supporters who were Aubrey's main concern, and he remembers them with affection.

'On the flights to Rotterdam I put one person on each flight – friends, family – and I gave them a free trip. I said, "You come along, but you've got to look after this group of people." We never had any problems with drink or loutism, because I think they were very pleased to be able to go and see another country. We had one bloke who was so excited he got on the wrong coach and he went up to Limburg. But that was very rare, everyone used to help each other. I suppose it's probably the same now, except for the yobs. We never had any of that, never any at all. There was an affinity – we were Spurs supporters. You'd sit there and talk about games from before the war. It was very new to all of us.'

Perhaps luckily, Aubrey never had the chance to deal with English fans as their reputation changed in Europe and, ironically, it was his pioneering work in flying supporters of the England team to games that led to a break in his love affair with the game.

'In 1966, I went to the World Cup,' he says. 'I felt very intimidated by it all – the nationalism frightened the life out of me. At times I thought I was at the Nuremberg Rally, the fervour of everybody. It wasn't really a game, it was a game they were watching, but they were fighting so much to win that it upset me so much that I've really fallen away. I go occasionally, but I'm 85 now, so I don't really want to get involved in anything like that.'

It's a sobering conclusion to a wonderful episode, and one that may be surprising to those of us raised on heady memories of English football's 'greatest day'. But let's remember Aubrey is a man who had grown up seeing and dealing with the results of the worst excesses of nationalism.

But what was it that made Aubrey get started on his European odyssey?

'I had a sense, and Sid Silver did too, we had a feeling that Spurs were going to do something. Don't forget, it was the first European competition, and nobody realised what it meant. It was a very exciting period.

'I had a feeling at the time that something special was happening, and that's partly what drove me. In a business sense I thought it was an opportunity, it's something that I know.' At this stage Aubrey casually drops in a piece of information that brings the story full circle. 'By 1965 my company was big enough to be taken over by Thomson's. I was first managing director of Thomson's. I'd been a cab driver until 1960. It was a particular thing at a particular time in history – it was a good time.'

It's difficult to imagine Daniel Levy or the current Thomson's board having much idea of just how deeply they were tapping into the club's roots when they signed their current sponsorship deal, or that the company they were signing a deal with owed so much to the efforts of a loyal Spurs supporter and canny businessman who once stood as a candidate for the Communist Party in east London.

Aubrey's connection with Spurs goes back a long way. 'It probably all started when I was about 12. I really was a keen supporter of Clapton Orient, but one Saturday my uncle took me to see Spurs play Arsenal at Highbury, and that was it – I'd never seen football like that before. Let me see, that would have been 1931.'

Like many of the supporters interviewed in this book, Aubrey's connection to the club doesn't come through a family tradition – 'My father wasn't much interested in football,' he remembers – but through a chance encounter with a side that captured the imagination.

At 85, Aubrey has understandably reined in his trips to watch Spurs, although his experiences at the 1966 World Cup and his awareness of the rise of hooliganism during the 1970s and 1980s means he has few regrets. You also pick up a little of the sense that he knows it's unlikely he'll ever see his team at such heights again, so why try to better what can't be topped? But once a Spurs fan, always a Spurs fan, and Aubrey hasn't lost the faith.

'Nowadays I go to the odd game,' he says, 'and most of my friends are Spurs supporters, so we talk. I'm not deeply involved, but the first report I look at is the Spurs, and the first result I look for is the Spurs.'

His favourite player, inevitably, comes from the 'Glory Days'. 'Tommy Harmer, I thought he was wonderful,' says Aubrey fondly. 'They talk about Beckham now, but Harmer could do it well before Beckham did. I loved to watch him. And Dave Mackay. Danny Blanchflower, I really thought he was something. Quite uncharacteristic when you talked to him. The others would all go out nightclubbing – they talk about the youngsters now, but the Spurs team then used to go out nightclubbing *before* the game. But not Danny.'

For Aubrey, the equation of Spurs with 'flash' has never quite rung true, at least for the side he remembers with greatest affection. 'Flash? Listen, Nicholson was one of the most sober managers there was. He never participated in any hullabaloo – it was difficult to get a comment out of him.

'Blanchflower was similar. He was highly intelligent, always reading, and he never mixed with the players socially, in any sense of the word. Yet on the field they accepted him. He never had to be one of the boys. Maybe the supporters were cocky, because we were riding high, but not to the point of being aggressive. I don't accept that they were flash.'

He's looked on with bemusement in recent years as the club has endured more than its fair share of trouble, trouble he puts down to what's gone on in the boardroom.

'Sugar saved the club, but it wasn't the club he was interested in, it was purely a commercial thing,' he says. 'Scholar and the others were Spurs supporters, but they didn't act that way. The main purpose of a football club is to entertain your supporters, but that's not what they did at all. At Spurs there's a very big gap between what the managements have delivered and what the supporters expect.'

Few expect to see the times Aubrey enjoyed again, and few could have expected what February had in store.

12

She wore a yellow ribbon:
Catherine Saunders

She wore, she wore
She wore a yellow ribbon
She wore a yellow ribbon in the merry month of May
And when, I asked, oh why she wore that ribbon
She said it's for the Tottenham and they're going to Wem-ber-ly
Wem-ber-ly . . .

The growth of live football on TV in recent years has led to a new stereotyped image for unimaginative studio directors. When all else fails, the camera focuses on depressed and sobbing fans who can always be called upon to provide the 'raw emotion' that programme makers deem so vital.

Any cameraman looking for a suitable 'misery' shot in February 2004 need only have set his equipment up at White Hart Lane. For no group of fans, surely, have been pushed to the limit of endurance and sanity than Spurs supporters were in one of the craziest months in the club's long, topsy-turvy history.

At 8.50 p.m. on 4 February, all seemed well. Spurs were 3–0 up against Manchester City in the FA Cup fourth-round replay, thanks to excellent goals from Ledley King, Robbie Keane and the returning Christian Ziege. The visitors were in disarray and were down to ten players. Home supporters were already looking ahead to the next round and an awayday at Manchester United; an hour later, they were pondering a visit to the Samaritans.

In what will no doubt become known as one of the FA Cup's most extraordinary games, destined to be pored over as long as the competition exists, Spurs somehow contrived to lose 4–3 to ten-man City, a team managed by Kevin Keegan, who, by his own admission, is no tactical genius; a team that hadn't won in the League for three months; a team that had lost Nicolas Anelka to injury in the first half and looked about as likely to score as Cliff Richard on a stag night.

Spurs, it has to be conceded, continued to create chances in the second half, striking woodwork and seeing City's keeper pull off a series of outstanding saves. However, in a display of defending that gave resonant new meaning to the word 'hapless', Tottenham suffered a collective dereliction of duty in protecting their lead. 'I don't believe that I'm seeing this,' said a clearly gobsmacked Andy Gray on Sky as City's winner was headed home by Jonathan Macken in the last minute; 'Tottenham just laid down and died,' denounced Alan Hansen on *Match of the Day*.

Tottenham fans, always quick to make their displeasure known, were too stunned to voice a reaction. That was saved for the morning after the nightmare before, as fans besieged the message boards and exchanged phone calls and text messages trying to make sense out of what had happened.

Anger focused on the players' unwillingness to offer some kind of explanation. Dean Richards, held by many to be the chief villain, refused to make any comment. Stephen Carr, the acting captain, rushed off without a word. It later transpired he had sped off to hospital to visit his wife, who had just given birth to their second child. Afterwards, Carr gave a clearly scripted and inane response on the official website about needing to 'bounce back', followed up by newspaper interviews a fortnight later in which he said 'it would be pointless apologising'. Only Johnny Jackson, a youngster with barely a handful of games to his name, offered even fleeting words of symbolic atonement.

Some fans demanded a written apology from the management and squad; others went mischievously further, arguing that before kick-off in the next game, at home to Portsmouth, the players' pay cheques should be put on a table in the centre circle, to test if any of the squad had the nerve to walk out and collect their money for services rendered.

Instead, Spurs served up another feast of comedy football, taking the lead three times against another hopelessly out-of-form team. As Pompey's third equaliser went in, some in the crowd turned, in the main against Dean Richards, who was loudly booed the next time he touched the ball.

Booing of home players is not unique to Spurs, but it appears to happen more often at White Hart Lane than at other grounds. Judging by the intensity of views expressed on the subject, the bulk of the crowd felt it was wrong to round on Richards, however badly he was playing. An answer of sorts was provided by the defender when he rose to head on a corner, enabling Gus Poyet – another target for the jeerers – to score with his knee, and thus secure yet another 4–3 scoreline, this time in Tottenham's favour.

Fans of a nervous disposition hoping for a boring 1–0 victory in the next game, against Champions League-chasing Charlton, were to be severely disappointed. Yet again, Spurs raced into a three-goal lead. Yet again, Spurs wobbled with only a late strike from Johnny Jackson making it 4–2 and putting an end to a spirited home comeback.

This was progress of sorts; the defending was more resolute and Richards in particular seemed to benefit from the generous encouragement from the visiting fans, giving one of his more commanding displays at the back. At the final whistle, the players joined in the celebrations with the jubilant travelling support, but their expressions seemed to suggest 'that showed you lot', rather than 'we're all in this together'.

One fan with a particular interest in Richards' reaction was Catherine Saunders. She was one of many moved to boo him during the Portsmouth game, and defended her right to express her view in such terms.

'He was one of our most consistent players, he was really solid; OK, he had a few bad games last season and you think he's just out of form, give him time. But this season it's just the huge difference. He's not man-marking, he seems really slow and doesn't know what he's doing. I thought maybe that when he came back from injury he'd be better, but he has just suffered a total lack of form.

'So it's not so much booing him personally as more, "Why is he in the team?" I can perhaps understand that for some players it would affect their confidence, but it was just a case of saying to David Pleat, "Get him off, sort his head out of whatever it is that is making him play so badly."

'Booing is not constructive and it's not something I would

generally do, but I really did think then that if Pleat hasn't noticed how badly Richards is playing then we have to draw his attention to it. He played well against Charlton in the next game and I heard he was taking the applause of the fans, perhaps in a kind of "up yours" way, but even if that was the case, then the booing worked and it made him play better. If the booing works, then we should boo him every week.'

A passionate response from a passionate fan. 'My boyfriend once asked me if I would miss a match to go out with him – I couldn't even believe he asked! He's not a fan; he likes football but doesn't support a team. It's a bit of a role reversal. I wouldn't go out with an Arsenal fan; well, I like to think so and it is one of the first questions I ask a bloke.'

If such fundamentalism is the true measure of the dedicated football fan then Catherine is a paid-up member of the zealots' club. A 26-year-old editor for a major publishing group in London, she may not fit the supporter archetype, but is as committed to her club as any other fan.

At face value, Catherine is one of the different breed of football supporters, the kind of walking marketing opportunity that has the moneymen positively drooling. She would be pigeon-holed by some of the old guard as one of the 'new, middle-class female fans', a label she is reluctant to accept, defining herself instead as a fan, pure and simple. Arguably, she is more demanding of decent facilities than her predecessors, and so to some she represents the kind of fan that has emerged since the year One BP (Before Pavarotti).

Appearances can be deceptive, however. Certainly, Catherine enjoys her creature comforts. 'Tottenham is not a nice area. The transport is terrible and the shops [laughs] . . . I often think I should be a Chelsea fan so at least I could get a Starbucks on the way to the ground. At Tottenham you can get a kebab, and that's about it.' Even so, anyone presuming that Catherine is one of the many thousands of indulged new converts jumping on football's popularity bandwagon would be mistaken.

She concedes that for some female supporters, especially, football's appeal has changed. 'I think maybe some women are perhaps more willing to go to games, with their partners or whatever. There are families who have been going together for a long time, so there are women who have been going since they were kids. But I think that because there is more glamour associated with football now, if a bloke was to ask a girl "Do you want to come to a match with me?" then maybe she is more likely to say yes now, maybe just to see what it's like.'

Catherine, however, needed no such outside encouragement in her own journey to becoming a fan. Born in Barnet, north London, she moved to Cornwall as a young child – a place that is some distance from White Hart Lane both geographically and environmentally.

'It's from when I was little. I can't really remember why I chose Spurs, I suppose it's a north London thing, but I can't remember it being a conscious choice. My friend's older brother supported Tottenham, so maybe he influenced me. None of my family really follow football, though I later found out that my granddad has been and is a fan in a fairly passive way.

'It intensified when I moved to Cornwall when I was eight. There were no local teams there and I continued to support Tottenham, that was around 1985–86. I used to keep in touch via the TV and my dad still worked in London so he used to bring home the *Evening Standard* on a Friday and I'd read through that.

'When I went to uni in Birmingham, I used to go to Spurs away matches in the Midlands. I actually chose my university on the basis of whether I'd be able to go and see Premiership football or not. I became a season-ticket holder when I moved back to London about four years ago.'

Catherine has become so dedicated that in some respects her life now revolves around Spurs. 'It's probably the most important thing, quite embarrassing, really. I always have the fixture list by my phone, so if anyone wants me to go out somewhere, I check that list first to make sure there's not a clash. I plan my holidays around football . . . the more you go the more involved you feel.'

So what kind of reaction does her devotion get from family and female friends? 'Most of the time they're quite amused by it, they don't really understand. There was a time on my sister's 21st birthday when Spurs were playing at home, and I went to the match. I went out with her afterwards, but sometimes they think it's a bit of a joke if I say I can't do certain things because Tottenham are playing.'

Catherine's introduction to Spurs came nine years ago. 'It was Spurs v. Man United in 1995. It took me a couple of years before I actually first saw them win; that was against Coventry and I was sitting in the Coventry end. I've been to so many diabolical matches, the first ten games I saw they lost. Still, I stuck at it.

'Jürgen Klinsmann was the player who stuck out, so did Teddy Sheringham. I was so gutted when he went to Man United. He'd been my favourite, but it wasn't like the Sol Campbell thing, that was obviously different.

'The experience did meet my expectations, though. The atmosphere was good and White Hart Lane is a really good ground. I still get that buzz even now. Because it is such a long walk from the Tube to the stadium it doesn't matter if I've had a really bad day at work or whatever, that trip to the ground cheers me up. It's letting off steam in some ways, and sort of, I don't know, maybe refocusing.'

As for many of her generation, unfortunately it is the frequent bad times that stick out. 'I can definitely say the worst one was the Man City Cup match this season. It was just horrible. I missed the League Cup semi-final against Chelsea when we won 5–1; I had a member's ticket at the time and I thought I can't face watching another pounding by them, but I did have a ticket for the FA Cup game a week later when they thrashed us 4–0. Just my luck.'

Given such a test of endurance, the obvious question is why she still goes. One of the criticisms aimed at 'new fans' is that they are glory-hunters who will not stay loyal to a losing side. To illustrate once more how she is not of that mentality, she gives a stout defence of principled support.

'I suppose it's the excitement and the knowledge that with Spurs you can never predict what might happen; we can always throw it away. When we played Birmingham City this season at home, we were 3–0 up at half-time, and I thought even then that we couldn't relax and just enjoy the game. It's the tension; you never feel comfortable because you just know that they can throw it away.

'You have to keep believing. You have to be an optimist, especially if you are a Tottenham fan. I've got a cousin who is ten and whose dad is an Arsenal fan. I really wanted him to support Tottenham, but I sometimes think, "Why am I doing this?" After the Man City game, I rang him up and said, "*Don't* support Tottenham – it's not worth it."

'I take some comfort in watching the young players come through and develop. Watching Ledley King play for England was great because I can remember when he first broke into the Tottenham team; he's always been skilful but not necessarily the most confident player.'

Faith in Tottenham's younger talents is not mirrored in her views on other players. Indeed it might be argued that Catherine's outlook lends itself to an attitude of the fan as 'consumer'; that, having paid a lot of money for the football 'product', supporters have every right to demand customer satisfaction and will speak out if they feel they are not getting their money's worth.

At least that is the perception of one kind of new-fan attitude. Catherine is definitely not sentimental when it comes to conventional thinking on the relationship between community and club.

'I don't have any attachment to the area at all – it's horrid, a complete dump. If they moved to Wembley, that would be great, but as long as it's north London that would be OK. It needs to be somewhere vaguely local, not like Wimbledon moving to Milton Keynes, which is just rubbish really.'

For some fans, such an attitude amounts to heresy. The more unreconstructed football bloke would put it down to her gender: 'What do women fans know about football in any case?' so the prejudice goes.

Catherine dismisses such a view, going on to deny that she has experienced any substantial hostility from male fans. 'I've always felt comfortable going to games. A few seasons ago when I didn't have a season ticket I would go on my own. To be honest, no one really takes much notice. I don't get any condescension or patronising attitudes as a general rule, at least not from season-ticket holders. Sometimes for cup games when tickets go on general sale you get people who only go a couple of times a season; they are the only ones who may be patronising – which is ironic as they are only armchair fans who only go occasionally.

'The only real comments I've had would be someone explaining to me something that has happened in a patronising way, stuff like that really.'

Troublemakers get shorter shrift. 'The ones that cause trouble don't really bother with the game, in my opinion, they're either watching the opposition fans or singing songs aimed their way. Where I sit is close to the away section and you see quite a lot of that. You get these blokes who are obviously, or rather maybe, don't have much money or that much in their life and they think that doing that or leading the chants makes them really important.'

On some counts, however, Catherine is a staunch traditionalist. There are the lucky clothes beloved of every truly superstitious fan – though with a nod to a woman's keener fashion sense she says, 'Those tight Kappa shirts and really fat blokes? Not a good thing.' In an age of quiet spectatorship, she is a fan who actually sings: 'That's one thing I'm a little embarrassed about because, naturally, my voice is higher and so it's taken me a few seasons to perfect my chanting rather than singing.' She is also a fervent believer in 'the Spurs Way' – 'That's why when GG [George Graham] was manager it just felt wrong. Players like Stephane Dalmat – OK, he's inconsistent, but that's the kind of player we want – are skilful, not afraid to take people on. We're not going to win games 1–0; it's more likely to be 4–3. Other clubs have proved you can play good football and still win.'

Catherine is not interested in those who may define her as a female supporter; she is a fan, plain and simple, with the same devotion to her club as even the most ardent male follower of Tottenham. She rejects the notion, for example, that the increase in the number of female fans in recent years has had any discernible influence on the behaviour of crowds.

'I don't think the idea that women "calm" male fans down is valid. There's always been kids around and that hasn't necessarily been a calming influence, so I wouldn't say women have had a real influence on the nature of the atmosphere at all. Though there was a funny incident after the Man City game when Dean Richards had been getting a lot of criticism and some guy shouted out, "Dean Richards is an effing you-know-what!" and then he said straight away to me, "Ooh, sorry, love." But that's the only time something like that has ever happened to me.'

Besides, for undeniable proof that she is cast in the Spurs-supporter mould, she has adopted that fatalistic, wry attitude that has come to mark out the devotees of the fading 'giant'. 'Spurs fans have to be nostalgic, really. There's nothing else to cling to. I'd like to see us win the League once in my lifetime; I'm not asking for them to win it loads of times, just once. But I think I might have to live for a long time.

'We need the right manager and the right structure at the club, and it would take a lot of work. I certainly don't think we are going to win it in the next ten years. Having a Director of Football doesn't seem to work, though it may be a personality thing. I just don't think he should have so much involvement as I don't think many managers would want to work in those circumstances; why do you need a manager if you have someone in that role?'

Despite her doubts about Tottenham's uniquely problematic management set-up, Catherine is cautiously optimistic about the future. While she retains a 'could do better' verdict on the board, she is prepared to accept that Daniel Levy is committed to the job in hand for the benefit of the club, though she scorns his rejection of Roman Abramovich in the summer of 2003.

Regarding the squad, she says, 'We have the basis for a really good team. It is positive, it's about getting the balance, the structure right and the right manager. We need a good motivator; what kind of team talk did they get at half-time against Man City? They do need someone to lead them on the pitch.

'I don't think Jamie Redknapp should be captain, I think that's more a PR thing. It's so frustrating. There are times when we play really well and it makes you really proud to be a Tottenham fan, and other times when we play so badly and it's just so humiliating.

'It would be nice to finish in the top half. In the next couple of seasons we should be getting into Europe. We have to stop being the kind of team that other sides think they've got a good chance of beating.

'I suppose the question is if we are a big club any more. A lot of fans still think that way. It baffles me when you see teams like Fulham and Charlton battling it out for fourth place and we're not; there's something wrong there. They have been five or so League places better than us, but I certainly think we are – or should be – a bigger club than Fulham or Charlton.'

13

Over land and sea: Jørgen Thue, Jesper Kristensen and Godfrey Gauci

We will follow the Tottenham
Over land and sea
We will follow the Tottenham
On to victory

With two straight League wins putting Spurs on the cusp of a European place by the middle of February 2004, it felt as if the ghosts of the Manchester City horror show had at least been laid to rest. It proved to be a temporary exorcism, however.

In the next game, at home against relegation-threatened Leicester, Spurs once again scored four goals; astonishingly – unbelievably – they also managed to concede four. The Foxes were another team in desperate straits, without a win in 14 games and the heart of their side staffed by Spurs cast-offs. Once more, Spurs were nigh-on unstoppable going forward, racing into a 3–1 half-time lead with goals from Michael Brown, Jermain Defoe and Robbie Keane.

Nonetheless, Spurs were occupying a football universe entirely of their own in which all the conventions of defending were turned upside down. As if to mimic the pantomime of the Manchester City game, the visitors also had a man sent off. Yet they established a 4–3 lead, thanks in the main to further comical mistakes by their opponents. This time Gary Doherty (twice) and Johnny Jackson were the main culprits. Doherty, affectionately dubbed the Ginger Pelé by supporters, was playing more like a ginger Ramon Vega.

The home crowd left the players in no doubt as to their feelings. Instead of haranguing individuals, the team and management were subjected to a collective jeer, though some, notably Defoe and Keane, were more likely excused. Put through the excruciating ritual of handing out and receiving the Man-of-the-Match champagne for the benefit of Sky afterwards, the pair looked suitably dismayed with the result. Keane, in particular, showed his maturity by keeping his obvious anger under wraps.

Keane and Defoe could be forgiven for raging at their colleagues, however. In four games Spurs had scored an astonishing 15 times. In normal circumstances, this attacking ambition would have had supporters fizzing with happiness, but such were the horrors at the back that once again the Tottenham supporter's lot was not a happy one.

Making sense of the nonsensical was proving difficult. The usual scattergun approach from some fans was a predictable response – sack the interim manager, sack the coach, sack Dean Richards, Gary Doherty or whoever was responsible for brewing the half-time tea. Following an assured international display at centre-half, most clamoured for the return of Ledley King to a defensive role, though mindful that in the past he had appeared just as jittery as his colleagues and that his prompting from midfield was instrumental in several goals.

The man making the crucial decisions, however, gave every impression of being just as stumped as his immediate predecessor. David Pleat wasn't scratching his head just yet, but his post-match press conferences throughout this extraordinary period were straying deeper into the surreal world the club now seemed to be operating in.

The Director of Football offered a whole stand-up routine of quips, gags and one-liners for a slightly befuddled media, suggesting that during the 11-day break after the Leicester game he would be visiting the doctors and taking plenty of aspirin.

Few fans were laughing, however, and it wasn't because of the way Pleat was telling them. He was in no position to complain, hoist by his own petard with the oft-stated principle that coaches should make do with what they have. It may not have been his squad, but whatever he was saying to them at half-time clearly wasn't working.

The pity was that such performances were clouding relative progress. The signing of Defoe, planned in advance or otherwise, was proving to be a masterstroke. He had scored four goals in just three games and Keane was proving equally prolific. Coupled with the return of Kanouté, Spurs now arguably had their most impressive forward line for a generation – certainly far better than the likes of Les Ferdinand, Steffen Iversen and Teddy Sheringham a little over a year before.

Results, too, were good; from looking like relegation material, Spurs were now reasonably placed to qualify for the UEFA Cup and were even being talked of as potential challengers for an unlikely qualification for the Champions League.

That was no comfort to the more critical fans among the support, especially those depressingly willing to boo their own players. But throughout this remarkable month, another aspect of Tottenham's support was confirmed. Crowds remained buoyant; indeed, just four days after the 'cup humiliation of the century', as the *Evening Standard* had it, 36,107 packed out White Hart Lane. If Spurs fans had had enough, they certainly were not showing it. And, extraordinarily, this team was not only still pulling in the crowds, it was pulling them in from across the globe.

Anyone who has been a regular visitor to top-flight football in the last couple of decades cannot have failed to notice the arrival of a new kind of supporter. Not the newly converted middle-class interloper resented by many of the old guard, or the 'family' fan with spouse and children in tow. Instead, the new arrivals can be distinguished chiefly by their language. They are fluent in all things to do with English football, but voice their support in a different tongue. Every weekend they arrive by boat and by plane from distant lands to the north. Like latter-day Vikings, they come to seek excitement and adventure in England, albeit without the rape, pillage and plunder. They are the Scandinavians.

No one is exactly certain when fans from Sweden, Norway and Denmark first started to come to games in England, but they have been a familiar presence at White Hart Lane for over twenty years. Among their number are two of the younger generation, Jørgen Thue, a 21-year-old from Bergen in Norway, and Jesper Kristensen, 24, from Copenhagen in Denmark.

It is little appreciated in Britain how popular the domestic game is in Scandinavia. Fans like Jørgen and Jesper will spend huge sums of money and devote whole weekends just to sit through 90 minutes of torture watching Spurs and Middlesbrough try to bore each other into submission.

We Are Tottenham

'I think a lot of British fans don't realise quite how into and informed of English football the average Scandinavian football fan is. It really has been fed to us since birth,' says Jørgen. 'It's the atmosphere, the pace and the traditional links it has to Norwegian TV; Saturday afternoon has been the equivalent of church time here since the 1970s.'

As everywhere, it is Manchester United, Liverpool, Arsenal and now Chelsea who tend to appeal to foreign fans, but Spurs still hold their own. Today, Tottenhams Venner, the Norwegian branch of the supporters' club, boasts over 3,000 members. In Denmark, Jesper is one among many Spurs fans planning to form their own supporters' club. 'Things are taking their time, but they have got interest from more than 1,000 people, so there's a healthy base here,' he says.

Quite why so many converts have been drawn to Tottenham is a remarkable testament to the power of television and the dedication of supporters who have no association with Tottenham, the club or area. It is also indicative of the more general appeal of the British game.

'I like the fan culture,' says Jesper. 'Also, the overall football culture shines through in ways which I doubt English fans even realise. Things like the hat-trick-scorer getting the match ball is unheard of here. In all honesty, Spanish football might just be more entertaining in certain respects, but the fighting spirit and tempo of the English game weighs heavier, in my book anyway.

'I started following Spurs in particular in 1993, when my whole family went to London for the first time. The first thing I did was go and buy a bunch of English football magazines. One story caught my eye. It was an interview with Ossie [Ardiles], who explained how he didn't just want to make Spurs win, but make them play attacking and entertaining football at the same time. He said how that had always been the way Spurs had played. I was deeply fascinated by this.'

Cost and the practicalities of living so far away preclude Jesper and Jørgen from making too many trips to White Hart Lane. In the main they rely on television for their Spurs fix. Jørgen catches around four or five live games a season, while a six-month stay in England a few years ago enabled Jesper to spend the best part of a season watching Tottenham in the flesh.

Starved of regular 'live' exposure to Spurs, Jørgen relies on the domestic online and print media that devote acres of print and web pages to English football. 'The media here in the most part focus on clubs with our players – Solskjær, Iversen, etc.,' he says. 'From just reading the papers you can keep pretty updated on things, and I stay in touch through the websites, but the general coverage of the Premier League is very good – too good, garnering much more attention than it really should get, to be honest.'

That criticism – that the domination of English football is at a cost to the indigenous Scandinavian game – is one Jesper echoes. 'Although I do follow the Danish league closely, I am by no means a fan of any team. There's not a real fan culture in Denmark as you see in England. This is why I support an English team, as the English fan culture is great.

'We've found this small pub owned by a Scottish Spurs fan. It's been made the "official" Spurs pub here in Copenhagen. But considering how many Spurs fans there apparently are in Denmark, it's amazing that there are usually only between ten and twenty fans there! A lot of people started supporting teams back when there was only one TV channel and the only foreign football on TV was English. For instance Leeds have quite a few fans here who started supporting them in the '70s.'

Whatever the rights and wrongs of the English influence, the Scandinavians seemingly cannot get enough of it. Jørgen's conversion began in the early 1990s, for reasons that he says are difficult to fathom now, but the presence of a compatriot in the Spurs ranks was a key influence.

'I really have no clue as to why I started to support Tottenham, but logic would say Erik Thorstvedt [the Spurs goalkeeper at the time]. All I know is that I was a huge fan of Lineker in the 1990 World Cup, plus Thorstvedt was my idol for all of my childhood and teens – the problem on all three accounts is that I cannot recall digging either of them before they got to Spurs.

'My first memory is the 1991 FA Cup semi, but by then I was well into the club. It was only years later I found out my uncle is a lifelong Spurs fan, so the only family influence that could have affected me never did. No one in my closest family likes football.'

Jørgen's commitment was cemented by a visit to White Hart Lane. 'It was versus Sheffield Wednesday in the fall of 1997. We were in crappy form, but won that game. It was an amazing experience from start to finish, the result of the game really not mattering at the end of the day. The Jumbotron took a while to get used to. The more I think of this, it was one of the more perfect experiences I've had as a football fan.

'I enjoyed the experience outside the stadium prior to kick-off, even though I was a bit overwhelmed by the whole society differentials from back home. We went early, as I have this fetish for sitting in a stadium and watching it fill up. Walking into White Hart Lane was mesmerising to say the least. It was beautiful. As for the crowd, they disappointed me a bit, and really just seemed like a bigger version of the football crowds back home, with the majority clapping politely and a small group in one section doing all the singing.

'Having said that, I was a little bit intimidated, but then again we were in a "kind" section. And by intimidated I don't mean anything negative happened, but rather that at 15 and in my first visit to England I hadn't quite come to terms with the foul-mouthed, in-your-face, working-class attitude over there. But I was never scared of hooliganism, going in or at any point during or after the game.

'The actual area was different. I don't really feel any attachment to the place. I've been there a couple of times, and on both occasions we basically ran to the stadium or shop and back out of there. It really felt like two different worlds, Tottenham and White Hart Lane. Quite frankly, the place felt intimidating on non-matchdays.'

Jesper had a similar introduction to the mean streets of London N17 – and to put to shame Tottenham fans who whinge about traffic problems that may add half an hour to their journey to the ground, he proved how Scandinavian Spurs will put up with considerably greater inconvenience.

'I was 16 when I experienced my first game; we had a trip on the boat that takes 18 hours. A Danish football and betting magazine arranges trips to England where you take the boat from Denmark to Harwich. The trip takes forever, so you leave Denmark on Friday, take the bus from Harwich to London, only get about an hour before the game and leave straight after. I had finally convinced my dad to go with me.

'Unfortunately the game was awful. We lost 1–0 to Leeds, back when Graham was their manager, and Allan Nielsen wasn't even playing. I was also somewhat disappointed with the atmosphere. As

I would later find out that was because the tickets included in the trip were in the West Stand.

'My first "real" experience was years later when I was living in London and had the chance to catch the atmosphere in the pubs beforehand and get tickets behind the goal. Very different experience, and it didn't hurt that I was there to witness Gazza's homecoming and Spurs beating Everton 3–2 after being down. The only other impression I remember is that the area struck me as being very run down.'

They share a love for Jürgen Klinsmann as the finest player they have seen in a Spurs shirt and both witnessed the solitary trophy haul of the last dozen years, when Spurs lifted the League Cup in 1999. Being so starved of success distinguishes Jørgen and Jesper from older supporters. As such, neither would be expected to indulge the emotional attachment to 'the Spurs Way' that Tottenham fans are wont to cherish, but Jesper is a firm believer in the club credo.

'We should always attempt to play our football with flair and be attack-minded, though you also need a sound defensive attitude to prevail in today's game, but it makes me very proud to be a Spurs fan.

'I would never sacrifice entertaining football for success altogether. It's very much possible to do both at the same time. The thing is though that some fans seem to think that both are immediately attainable. You need to have a period where you might have to sacrifice the entertainment a bit, get the defence stabilised. Once that is done you can much better afford to play flair football and still win.'

Jørgen's view is more pragmatic. 'I think the opinion of what the Spurs Way is supposed to be in this day and age now differs so much that it's all becoming kind of blurry anyway. I believe in playing the style of the manager, not the club.

'I guess it does annoy me, as football evolves, holding on for dear life to traditional ways of playing if it gets you nowhere – look at the Italian teams in Europe in the late '90s/early 2000s. And if all that's left of "the Spurs Way/Glory, Glory Game" that we can be proud of now is that it's *entertaining*, then there really isn't anything "Spurs" about it. It's not like our club invented fancy pansy football.'

Both Jesper and Jørgen are Spurs fans for life now. Jørgen has been quick to pick up what that support requires: 'We're world champions at satire and self-irony. That's what this club does to you.' Like

171

Jørgen, Jesper has declined to join any overtly 'political' supporter groups. 'They can be a good thing to get the fans heard. But I sometimes get the impression that they speak for a minority, and a minority with unrealistic opinions and demands. All the underachieving seems to have left many Spurs fans forever negative about almost anything at the club.'

This is not to say that Jesper does not share the sentimental attachments that British fans have, but he is distanced enough not to let that cloud his judgement as to what may be best for Spurs: 'I think I feel less for White Hart Lane as a stadium than people who have been there to see us win our greatest games. But I do feel that it's important to keep the club feeling alive, and staying put is part of that. So *if* we can stay while expanding the stadium we should do this. I do, however, realise that expanding the stadium is perhaps not possible. If the choice is between getting ourselves a real chance of success and staying at White Hart Lane, I'd say we'd have to leave. And I do think most fans will feel the same in the end. We cannot keep having a full house at 36,000 and refusing to move, while other clubs are having 60,000 plus every week.'

In some quarters of Tottenham's support, that is not a popular view, but, in general, Jesper says he has been well received by his British counterparts. 'I think some British fans view foreign fans as not quite real fans because we have no real relation to London. In some cases rightfully so because a few fans say, "I'm a fan of Spurs but also this team in my country, this team in Italy, this team in Spain", etc. Personally I hate that, and I do feel that I get more respect when I mention that my only other team is Spurs reserves and I've lived in London.'

For Spurs to maintain that global appeal, however, form surely has to pick up. So, what of the present and future? Jesper says, 'I think we've got something big building. Lots of good promise in the team all over the park. We need to improve in a few positions, but once that's done, the sky's the limit in my honest opinion.

'The next few years will allow the new owners to find the club its niche under their ruling. But I don't think I'll live to experience Spurs as a constant top team in England and Europe.'

Starved of seeing Spurs land the glittering prizes, Jørgen and Jesper are foreign fans who have an understandably rather world-weary view.

One overseas Spur who has had the privilege of seeing a successful Tottenham side is Godfrey Gauci. A 64-year-old accounting teacher at a sixth-form college, he is one of a sizeable number of Tottenham supporters from Malta.

This tiny Mediterranean island has long been an outpost of Spurs support, a reflection of Malta's close ties with Britain in general and with football in particular. The whole island famously won the George Cross in recognition of the bravery of its people during the Second World War; wags would say the island's Tottenham fans should have a gong struck in their honour for what they have had to put up with over the years, but Godfrey is nothing if not a true believer.

'I first started following Spurs in 1960 and at that time it was not a difficult choice because Tottenham were playing an effervescent type of football. Manchester United were enormously popular on the island at that time (they still are!), but as far as I was concerned there has only been one option.'

There is a long-established Spurs supporters' club in Malta, sited in Frederick Street in the capital, Valletta. Membership stands at over 800 – not bad going for a country with a population of just 391,000 and a place where not just British but also Italy's major clubs vie for the affections of the population.

'The youngest member is a few months old and the oldest over 70,' says Godfrey. 'The club is open every day and members and non-members congregate there for a drink and to relive football matches, recent ones and not so recent ones. Each one of us has opinions about what should or should not be done for the club to move forward, but one common factor is that we are all extremely hungry for success.'

There are also regular live TV games to enjoy, but watching Spurs used to require much greater effort when Godfrey first started following them.

'There was no Sky television in those days, of course, and we had to rely on the World Service, newspapers and the occasional game on TV. I first came to White Hart Lane in 1963 and most of the ground was standing room only. I misjudged distances and times and I arrived about 30 minutes before the game was due to start and the ground was already completely full. The ticket attendant refused me permission to enter. "The ground is full," he said. "But you can't do that to me!" I said. "I have come all the way from Malta, and that's about 1,500 miles just to watch my Spurs! I'm new here, I lost my way, blah, blah, blah, you must understand and help me out, blah, blah, blah . . ." It must have been my lucky day because I had picked the right turnstile. He told me that he had seen war service on the island and to my obvious relief he relented and let me in; free of charge too, if my memory serves me right.'

Godfrey became a relative regular thereafter, travelling to London every August specifically to watch football matches, and Spurs in particular when they were playing at home.

But the gradual decline that has set into the club means it is harder for Tottenham to attract a new generation of fans, at home and abroad. The familiar factors in recruitment to the cause still hold true in Malta according to Godfrey – family associations, Tottenham's reputation for flair football and even 'because one of my colleagues at work whom I don't particularly like supports Arsenal.

'Our cause has not been helped by the lack of silverware and some crap performances which we put up when games were being shown live on Sky. One that comes to mind was when we played Ipswich away a couple of years ago and George Graham was the manager. I just couldn't stand it any more and switched the set off. Apparently I was not the only one to be disgusted because later in the week Graham apologised to the travelling supporters.

'I try my best to generate support for Tottenham in the classroom. When I first started as a young primary school teacher in 1958, it was not a difficult task because Spurs were a very successful side then and riding the crest of a wave. I occasionally meet students from those days and they tell me that I am to blame for all the pain they have gone through in recent years!

'Spurs have lost their way in the last ten years or so and for this reason I have been less successful in recruiting new fans. As an accounting teacher I frequently have to come up with names for questions which I devise involving sole traders, partners, or limited companies; things like "Ledley King, a sole trader", "Richards and Carr are business partners", that sort of thing. Late last year when Spurs were in the relegation zone, the wittiest student in my class sent an SMS message to all his classmates suggesting that the name of the question which they had to hand in the next day for marking should be changed to "White Heartache PLC". Whenever there's a particularly bad result for Spurs, my students examine me very closely on my entry into the lecture room to judge my mood.'

Despite all the doom and gloom, however, Godfrey's enthusiasm is undiminished; indeed, he is more positive about the future than he has been for some time. 'I really do believe that things are looking much brighter,' he says.

There was time to ponder if that was the case for both fans and players as Spurs now had a week and a half until their next game. The club took the chance to take the players for a bonding trip to Dubai – just the place to gear up for an evening match in Middlesbrough. A flat display on Teesside ending in a 1–0 defeat didn't suggest an awful lot had been gained – although conceding only one goal could be seen as a bit of a result for Tottenham's defence.

Another break, this time of two weeks, gave the club plenty of time to focus on what was needed for the rest of the season. Such was the state of the table that a decent run could still secure the European place that Spurs had been vainly grasping at for the past few seasons. Opponents Newcastle had European ambitions of their own, eyeing fourth place and a Champions League spot, so a lively game was anticipated, all the more so when David Pleat unveiled a starting line-up in which Freddie Kanouté, Jermain Defoe and Robbie Keane formed a three-pronged attack. But a match that had promised a hatful of goals produced only one, and that when Newcastle's Andy O'Brien put it through his own net.

Tottenham visited unhappy hunting ground Old Trafford as Manchester United were enduring what was for them a slump. But over the years Spurs have developed a specialist service in helping teams end runs of bad form, and did so again. Pleat reverted to 4–4–2, claiming three strikers would unbalance the team, and handed a start to raw youngster Dean Marney. Tottenham's usual cautious and unconfident approach away from home saw them go down 3–0 to a United side that didn't have to try too hard. Watching Spurs on the road was becoming a grim affair, and the team's next destination was St Mary's, Southampton, a stadium at which they'd never scored. Another bad sign was that the Saints had a new manager, and the Spurs assistance package also included a clause that almost guaranteed a result to a new boss. True to form, Spurs lost 1–0.

So, after the fireworks of February, March had turned into a damp squib. In four games Spurs had scored only one goal, and that by an opposition player. Tottenham's notoriously lightweight midfield meant that they couldn't make the quality up front count. As the season petered out, the only point of interest remained speculation about the identity of the new manager. And there seemed to be dark clouds gathering here too.

14

Be an Arsenal fan: Tom Watt

My old man
Said be an Arsenal fan
I said f . . .

For some time, Giovanni Trapattoni had been widely assumed to be the man Tottenham had secured to be the new manager – although much of the press comment on the issue consisted simply of running a few names as possibles without any real evidence. The latest batch of speculative stories seemed to suggest that 'Trap' was not the done deal the club had led everyone to believe. Some said that he wanted to stay on as coach of Italy, while other stories suggested he had refused to work with David Pleat deciding transfer policy. When the storm over Chelsea's courting of England boss Sven-Goran Eriksson broke, it prompted a fresh bout of speculation linking incumbent Chelsea coach Claudio Ranieri with the Spurs job. Then Raddy Antic, Pleat's old friend, resigned from Celta Vigo after a short but unproductive spell in charge there. Could he be the new man after all? The Pleat conspiracy theories cranked into gear once more. Names began to eddy around dizzyingly: José Mourinho, Fabio Capello and then, extraordinarily, Hull City's Peter Taylor. Based on the admittedly unscientific theory that there's no smoke without fire, Spurs fans were increasingly convinced that the board was no closer to sorting the management situation than it had been eight months before.

It didn't help that, in the middle of all this, new season-ticket prices were announced. Most of the increases were fairly low, and pressure from the Supporters' Trust had secured the return of some of the lost benefits – although some supporters expressed anger that the club was presenting the return of things it had taken away as 'new' – but many more asked how they could be expected to renew when they didn't know what they would be getting, or, with Spurs plummeting down the table, what division they'd be playing in. Indications from the club were now that the manager issue wouldn't be resolved until well into the summer. Having just announced that income from ticket sales and merchandising was significantly down on previous years, the Spurs board was playing with fire.

Spurs were being dragged into a relegation battle and anger inevitably focused on the man most visibly in charge – David Pleat. As caretaker manager, he had been responsible for team selection and tactics. As Director of Football, and so an executive director of the board, he'd overseen the assembly of the squad for five years. Many fans reasoned he should shoulder some responsibility. If not, then what was he actually doing in such a senior position?

In Pleat's defence, this was still Glenn Hoddle's squad, a fact that should not have been lost on those claiming Hoddle should never have been sacked back in September. And what of the players, who had reportedly wanted shot of Hoddle and his tactics but who now, having got their wishes, were still not delivering?

But just like Hoddle, Pleat was making things very difficult for even his staunchest supporters. His press statements were increasingly defensive, but as Spurs prepared to face Chelsea he shocked many with an inflammatory outburst that had him sounding more like Alf Garnett than a football manager. Railing against foreign footballers and coaches, he told *The Express*: 'Chelsea are a bought team and apart from John Terry and Frank Lampard, they are a bunch of immigrants. I like a level playing field and there's a morality issue here.' He went on to claim foreign coaches were 'gypsy-like in their mentality. They are a different breed and whether this is a good thing for the English game, I don't know.'

Aside from the obvious errors of fact, Pleat was straying into dangerous territory. By all accounts, he is a good-natured man with a mischievous wit, but if he was cracking jokes this time they were in poor taste. Using such loaded language at a time when the serious issue of immigration was so raw was at best ill-advised and at worst utterly irresponsible.

Pleat was doubly damned. In one fell swoop he had virtually trashed the idea of Spurs appointing a foreign coach – including his good friend, the Serbian Raddy Antic. And what message was Pleat sending out to prospective foreign buys, including Dutchman Mark van Bommel and the Brazilian prodigy Diego?

By now the press were beginning to tire of the charade to name the new manager. What had started off like a jovial game of Cluedo between Pleat and his media interrogators as to the mystery man's identity was now turning into an endless game of Mornington Crescent – a game of barely understood rules with no conclusion in sight.

To no one's surprise, Spurs lost to a Chelsea team which didn't have to expend too much energy ahead of their Champions League clash with Arsenal, a quarter-final clash which further emphasised how far down the pecking order Spurs were in London. The 0–1 scoreline also meant it was six weeks since a Spurs player had scored a goal.

Respite seemed in sight with a Good Friday visit to Everton, for whom Spurs have proved a bogey team in the Premiership. Instead, once again for the benefit of Sky's live audience, Spurs delivered what *The Independent* described as 'a performance which shamed the once proud name of Tottenham Hotspur', losing 3–1.

Two days later, as Spurs stumbled clumsily to a 1–1 draw with struggling Manchester City, the calls for Pleat's head rang out from the stands. Pleat claimed, bizarrely, that it wasn't personal, and that as he was 'the acting manager, I don't know what they are worried about'.

It was desperate stuff both on and off the pitch, and Spurs travelled to Bolton for a game no one expected them to win, with pundits on that morning's *TalkSport* preview describing a bet on Bolton to win as like getting 'free money'. They were right: Spurs surrendered 2–0. Pleat's comment afterwards was, 'Some of my players play for pride, but others play for money.' If this was meant to motivate his players, it seemed an odd way to do it. Pleat appeared, once again, more interested in avoiding any personal blame than in finding a way to get the best out of his limited resources.

With the media searching for new metaphors to evoke the sheer ineptitude of the team and club, issues began to unravel. As season-ticket renewal packages arrived on fans' doormats, the Supporters' Trust sent a restrained but charged letter to Daniel Levy. It made a salient point highlighting that the club had refused to budge on extending the deadline for season-ticket renewals, citing the need for 'long-term planning', something which sat uneasily with the eight-month search for a new boss. It continued, 'In February, David Pleat said the new manager was "done and dusted"; he is now quoted as saying he is "scouring Europe" for the new man. Mr Pleat's statements are contradictory and we urge you to be open with supporters about whether a firm appointment has been secured and, if not, when it is realistically envisaged.'

It also addressed one of the more persistent and worrying rumours about the management saga. 'The media continues to speculate that prospective candidates are either reluctant to commit or reluctant to work alongside Mr Pleat. At the AGM in December, you said you were, "100 per cent behind David Pleat". Are you therefore only prepared to hire a manager who will work with Mr Pleat as Director of Football?'

The letter, although critical, was still worded constructively, and drew widespread approval, even from those Spurs fans who had seen the Trust as too willing to toe the Enic line. But Daniel Levy, always a private man reluctant to step into the limelight, broke cover with a petulant reaction which betrayed the disarray at the most senior levels of the club.

'I have publicly stated the case on the timing of the announcement of a new manager and I have nothing further to say on this,' he began curtly, before continuing, 'The public nature of your letter has led to adverse media comment, the publicity of which is damaging to the club and counter-productive. I think we should review all matters when we meet.'

The implication was clear – Levy was only prepared to work with the Trust if it sold his line to the fans. Once it had spoken on behalf of the fans, he would ask for his ball back.

It all added up to a worsening situation on and off the pitch, something Tottenham fans were becoming wearily used to. But there was support for them from a surprising source, a fan of rivals Arsenal.

'There's that whole thing about Spurs fans that they moan all the time,' says Tom Watt. 'I tell you what, though: the ground's always full. I just look at how the club has been run down the years and you just think, Spurs supporters deserve more than that.'

Tom is a broadcaster and author, and more recently David

Beckham's ghostwriter. He is renowned as a considered, articulate and passionate Arsenal fan who has written extensively on his club. Others will remember him as an actor, notably playing Lofty, one of the mainstays of the early years of the BBC soap *EastEnders*. Few, however, will recognise him as a stalwart defender of the Tottenham supporters' cause.

His ability to ignore the more petty aspects of club rivalries means he can see fans for what most of them are: loyal and committed individuals with a genuine love for the game, whatever their particular club. To back his views up he has personal experience of what it means to be a suffering Spurs fan.

'Even though the rivalry between Spurs and Arsenal is as bitter as any in football,' he says, 'aside from the nutters, by and large football supporters are football supporters.

'I remember one night a few seasons back – I don't know why I was there – but I went to St James's Park and it was when [Tottenham] got done 6–1. Where I was sitting was right behind the Tottenham fans. Once the second or third goal went in, I started to have a chat with a few Spurs fans and there's me, an Arsenal supporter, getting angry at what I was watching, thinking, "These fans have come all this way, a 700-mile round trip, and they deserve better than this."'

It's not the first time that Tom has sprung to the defence of Tottenham's maligned followers. As a presenter on BBC Radio London and in numerous contributions to football debates on other stations such as Radio 5 Live, whenever the subject of Spurs has come up, Tom has come to the supporters' defence. His is one of the few voices to be heard rising above the general bluster and fierce antagonism that has defined the intense rivalry between the capital's traditional big guns.

This is not to say that Tom is immune to the attractions of such a longstanding feud – but he's not one to wallow in smug satisfaction at the contrasting fortunes of the two clubs.

'I think in a way, I kind of preferred it when the rivalry was a bit closer, really, in terms of how the teams perform. It's a bit like how it was when I was an Arsenal fan when I first started watching; then it was like, "Oh, we beat Tottenham, so nothing else in the season matters." It's a bit similar at Tottenham now – it doesn't matter what has happened in the rest of the season just so long you get a result at Arsenal.'

We Are Tottenham

Perhaps the reason for Tom's view stems from his own long experiences of supporting his club. Tom is old enough and wise enough to know that fortunes change; in contrast to the younger generation of Arsenal fans who have known only almost unbroken success, Tom remembers a different era – when it was Spurs who held sway, not just in London, but in the country as a whole.

He grew up on Caledonian Road, deep in the heart of Arsenal country, and just round the corner from where Charlie George lived. Inevitably, Arsenal was his chosen club and he began visiting Highbury in the mid-1960s. 'It was always going to be Arsenal – although, to be fair, at that time there were plenty of people who went to Tottenham, the glory-hunters, you know.

'We're talking about the greatest Tottenham team of all, so there were plenty of people even from my part of Islington which was bang on Arsenal's doorstep, a lot of people who followed Spurs then. Though, to be truthful, that was still a time when a lot of people still went to watch both clubs, because you could just turn up and get in. Spurs then, though, they basically were the big bollocks.'

Talking bollocks is the more familiar phrase that springs to mind if any Spurs fan makes claims for similar high status these days. Tom's comments are a stark reminder of how far the club's stock has fallen, but his evaluation of the differences between the two sides almost forty years ago is based on factors other than straightforward success.

'I don't think there was quite the same importance applied to the way the teams "traditionally" played. It was more about "We're from Holloway and you're from Tottenham." It was more to do with genuinely a local rivalry rather than a clash of styles, although that obviously was there. That Spurs Double team was arguably one of the most stylish sides ever seen. Although they weren't all about style with people like Dave Mackay and Bobby Smith in the side, they could put it about a bit, but that wasn't the big deal. Nowadays people would probably talk more about the different styles, but then it was all about neighbourhood and territory.

'A lot of people my age who were going then – I was about 13 – they've moved out to Hertfordshire, moved away from where they grew up, though that was already happening then so maybe that has got something to do with it. Maybe the boroughs in London don't have the same identity that they used to. At Arsenal at that time you had different little groups – Holloway, Highbury, people from outside the immediate area like mobs from Burnt Oak, Cricklewood, Archway, so it was much more that you grew up in your little patch, and then your little patch spread on the North Bank or wherever you were. But then Tottenham was another patch altogether.

'Back then you noticed the territorial difference more. The trip up the Seven Sisters Road was a trip up to bandit country and I'm sure it was the same the other way round. One night in 1968–69 I was on the Paxton Road, it was heaving, absolutely heaving, and hooliganism was starting then, although trouble between Arsenal and Tottenham goes back to the 1920s.'

Mention of that season in the late 1960s prompts Tom to consider how and when things began to change and the balance of power swung in Arsenal's favour. He can even pinpoint the exact game when he believes the tide turned, when Arsenal began to seriously challenge their rivals and set the two clubs on the different courses that have led to what is essentially a role reversal.

'I guess the thing that really did it, and I think did it long term, was that the balance of power in north London shifted over the two legs of the League Cup semi-final. It was 1968–69: first game was at Arsenal, we won 1–0 through John Radford, the most route-one goal you've ever seen in your life; and then the return at Spurs, that was the most violent game of football I've ever seen in my life. It was unbelievable, I mean it was just people you would never imagine – Alan Gilzean going over the ball on the goalkeeper, that sort of thing. And people make a fuss of what happened at Old Trafford last September!

'But anyway, in the return Radford scored an equaliser and we were through to the final. Fat lot of good it did us because we lost in the final to Swindon, but that night, something changed because it was still a great Spurs side; people like Greaves, and Gilzean, Mike England, Pat Jennings in goal. Without being probably as good a footballing team, we were stronger. And it's never been quite the same since. I've always thought that since then Arsenal were more likely to win the League, whereas ten years previously it was Spurs.'

Up until the late 1980s, relative parity existed between the two clubs, but the gap that Arsenal began to prise open around that time has widened to what some believe is an unbridgeable chasm. Before Arsenal embarked on a reign of success initiated by George Graham, it appeared Tottenham would be the club to forge ahead, emboldened by a young, dynamic board prepared to think big and spend big, in contrast to the rather fusty, backward-looking old guard at Highbury. So, from a Tottenham point of view, what went wrong?

'I think it's entirely down to how the clubs have been run, there is no other explanation for it really,' Tom says. 'I think in the last 15 years the difference has been between Irving Scholar turning Spurs into a PLC, which probably seemed like a good idea at the time, but it took the club out of the hands, strictly speaking, of football people. Whereas Arsenal haven't gone that route. They've stuck with football people and as a club they've stuck with football business. If you get the football right, then the business follows. If you try, as Tottenham did, to run a business with a travel company and kit manufacturer and all that other rubbish off the back of a football club, it ain't gonna work.

'At Arsenal there's a very strong sense of the past. And it's funny, when I first started watching Arsenal I think there was a sense of that holding us back. Billy Wright was the manager and it wasn't until 1970 that I saw them win a trophy and that was after 18 years of potless football. But I think now and in more recent years that sense of tradition has been a very good thing. It's kept Arsenal in touch with what matters in football.'

Dissenters cite that far from having differences, there were more similarities between the powers-that-be of both clubs, particularly in the make-up of their young, dynamic figureheads, Irving Scholar and David Dein.

The theory that Scholar and Dein are cut from the same commercial cloth is not one Tom subscribes to. 'Where David Dein's concerned, an outsider might say that. The difference is that the club was always bigger than David Dein. I've got a lot of time for him; I think he's done a really good job. Rather than saying, "Right, here's my vision and I'm going to impose that on the football club," what he's done is he's let the club get to him; he's absorbed what the club's been about. There have been mistakes, don't get me wrong, but by and large, David has had people on the board who've been around a lot longer than he has; he's listened to them.'

Maybe an analysis such as that points up one of the fundamental differences between the two clubs. Alan Sugar was detached from the club and misunderstood what made Spurs tick, reacting to circumstances rather than dictating them, chopping and changing managers in ever more desperate attempts to deliver on his promises.

The contrast with Arsenal in this context is a stark one. 'One of the reasons George Graham built a successful side,' Tom says, 'is that he had the benefit of time and stability. That's been the key. In the roughly forty-odd years I've been a fan, essentially we've had four managers – Bertie Mee, Terry Neill, George Graham and now Arsène Wenger.'

While he is enjoying his team's success, there is regret on Tom Watt's part that the game he has followed for so long has become so predictable. 'I think it's football in general now; until this season and the extraordinary circumstances of what's happened at Chelsea, basically since the mid-1990s, in terms of the domestic game there's been only two clubs – Man U and Arsenal, and that's it; the rest are also-rans. Yeah, it's great to be one of those two clubs, but it would be better if there were more in the running.'

Asked if there is a possibility of other clubs, specifically Spurs, catching up, he says, 'I don't think there's a cat in hell's chance. The only chance is that, say, for whatever reason, Arsenal fall behind. Obviously I don't think that will happen and I hope it won't happen, but it would be conceivable that Arsenal could go backwards.'

So there is hope. 'If Spurs turned round and appointed the right manager for instance, they could win the League – conceivably with the right manager that may happen because George [Graham] didn't really spend a lot of money and neither, really, has Arsène Wenger. To win the League first time round Wenger inherited Graham's defence and Bergkamp, but he spent little, under £10 million, which conceivably is the kind of money you could spend now to do well in the League.

'But looking at it logically, there's more chance of Arsenal falling behind because of the stadium thing getting out of hand. And Wenger deciding to leave.'

So can a club starved of success for so many years keep on pulling in successive generations of supporters, when their neighbours can offer a more tempting proposition? 'I don't know about that,' Tom says. 'I don't think for Spurs that's a major problem. I think it has enough about it with the people that follow the club; they will follow it passionately enough for it to be passed on. The problem, I think, is the same at Arsenal in that you lose a generation because they can't get in or afford to get in the ground. Ticket prices are outrageous and are putting potential supporters off.'

Spoken like a true Spurs fan.

15

The famous Tottenham Hotspur: Norman Jay

We're the famous Tottenham Hotspur
and we're going to Wem-ber-ly

Spurs fans had approached the first north London derby of the season with trepidation, but with the return looming the mood was close to despair. Arsenal were unbeaten all season and generally acknowledged to be playing the finest football seen for years in England. A win could see them claim the title at White Hart Lane, and plunge Spurs into deep relegation trouble, and the formbook made this look like a bout between Mike Tyson and Lily Savage.

When Arsenal scored with their first counter-attack after three minutes, simply running through Tottenham's excuse for a midfield and slicing the hapless defence apart, the stage looked set for the biggest humiliation yet. Arsenal's 2–0 lead at half-time didn't begin to tell the story of the dominance they'd enjoyed. Some home supporters headed for the exits – the ultimate expression of how little confidence they had in their side even in this vital game.

Somehow, though, Spurs came out fighting. It was later reported that, during the interval, David Pleat had fooled the players into thinking that a 'famous Italian coach' had taken his seat in the directors' box, when it was, in fact, a plant – an occasional driver of the team coach who apparently bears an uncanny resemblance to a certain foreign boss. Whatever the truth of Pleat's half-time rallying call, it worked; Spurs pulled a goal back after a fine strike by the much-maligned Jamie Redknapp, whose hopeless attempt to stem the tide for Arsenal's first goal had evoked memories of Terry

Fenwick attempting to stop Maradona in the 1986 World Cup finals. Arsenal had taken their foot off the gas a little and, roared on by some incredible home support, Spurs were at least attempting to take the game to them. In the final minutes of the game a tussle between Arsenal goalkeeper Jens Lehmann and Robbie Keane led to tumultuous scenes in the Arsenal box and the referee stepped in. After what seemed an age, he pointed to the spot and White Hart Lane erupted. Keane kept a cool head in the most heated of moments and slammed the ball home before launching into his trademark goal celebration, somersaulting in front of the delirious Spurs fans in the Paxton Road end.

Seconds later the final whistle went, heralding some of the strangest scenes ever seen at the famous old ground. Spurs fans danced and cheered wildly as their players punched the air, while away in the visitors' section of the Park Lane stand Arsenal fans launched their own celebrations at gaining the point they needed to clinch the title after second-placed Chelsea had lost their game that morning.

Never can a north London derby have ended with both sets of fans so happy. But while Arsenal had the achievement of another title, the second to be secured under the noses of the old enemy, the context of Spurs fans' celebrations was that a shred of dignity had been maintained. For many supporters, that was not good enough.

Two days after Arsenal confirmed their League title, and after a week of warm weather, the heavens opened and London was being deluged in a torrential downpour. Sitting in an office underneath the Westway in Notting Hill, one of Tottenham's most famous and well-liked celebrity fans was in a suitably downcast mood.

'Look at how much quicker Arsenal were,' said Norman Jay, MBE, pioneering DJ of international repute, and now simply a fan raking over the disappointments of the season. 'They are athletes, they are comfortable on the ball, everyone knows what they should be doing. We are always struggling, getting caught in possession, closed down every game.

'If we'd lost that game, the humiliation would have been too much. I was there in '71 when they did it before; I bunked off school to go. I even saw them beat Liverpool to do the Double 'cos we bunked into Wembley. It's come back to haunt me: here I am, a 40-

something season-ticket holder and I'm watching them do that to us on our pitch.'

'That night I was doing my show on GLR. I have quite a lot of banter on the radio, but I studiously avoid talking about football: it's not a football show and it's not a talk show. That night, I knew London was listening and there was a pause before I started – a pregnant pause, waiting for me to say something about it. In the end I said, "I'm not here to face the music – I'm here to play the music."'

For Norman, the joy of Robbie Keane's penalty equaliser had proved short-lived. While the point had virtually guaranteed Tottenham's Premiership survival, the inquest into a pitiful season had begun in earnest among the club's fans.

Tottenham fans do not come more earnest or committed than Norman: he is a self-confessed Spurs fanatic. While other celebrity fans – and Spurs have more than their fair share – wear their club colours as a PR exercise to ingratiate themselves with the masses, Norman is the real deal. In the aftermath of one of the most disappointing seasons for Spurs in over 20 years, he is visibly angry at how his experience of football has altered for the worse.

'Things have changed, for everyone. The whole raison d'être for going to football has altered. I feel ripped off, undervalued, alienated. I could turn round and say, "You know what, I don't support this team any more", but you can't. It's not like changing your shoes, your car or even your girlfriend. They know they have this grip on you. It's not just Spurs, it applies to all fans, it's a generational thing. If I was 20 years younger, I'd be just a spectator.

'But we're of that generation who are fanatical. We don't have that attitude of "Yeah, they're winning today, let's support them," whereas in five years' time if they are doing badly, they'll stop going. They have no emotional attachment. I wish I could do that now, honestly, because our generation of fans are neglected.'

Despite his obvious disenchantment, Norman still goes to as many games as time and his work commitments allow. It is just that, acutely aware of the sacrifices supporters make and the rewards footballers now enjoy, results matter much more than they perhaps once did.

'It's a different era and it makes a difference. When it cost you a quid to get in and you were part of a 60,000 crowd, you were much more tolerant, but not now, no way. Not when you're paying £40 it's not, and they're not making the effort. Players should be booed. We cheer them when they're doing well, so why not boo them when they're doing badly? Personally, I don't, but you have to let them know if they're not up to scratch – he who pays the piper calls the tune. If you haven't got much money and you are paying that much to see them perform that badly, you have every right to dig 'em out.

'The players don't care; they don't have anything to do with you. They're just someone you see on the telly and in the programme; they don't care just as long as they get their money. If there was a direct correlation between how you perform and what you receive, you'd soon see them buck their ideas up. If I don't perform, I'm out of work. You're only as good as your last game or your last gig – there's no difference.'

By way of illustration, Norman relates how, running to catch a flight for a gig in Newcastle straight after Spurs had lost 4–0 at home to Chelsea, his phone rang. '"All right, Norm?" It's a Spurs player ringing me up, a footballer with a lot of Premiership experience. "I'm having a party in a couple of weeks, I hope you can do it", all bright and breezy. And I thought, "You fucking tosser. That says it all about you. You've just been stuffed 4–0 and you're thinking about having a party." If I had no legs, I'd still run around for that team. I'm sure out of a 36,000 crowd there must be kids sitting there who'd fucking die for that shirt and there's people who are wearing that shirt earning 20 or 30 grand a week and all they're interested in is that they've got their first-team bonus.

'I don't begrudge them their money as long as they earn it. It should be performance-related. It's like anything, if you perform well, the world's your oyster; when you don't, prepare to get nothing. There has to be an element of hunger, but when you're comfortable there's little incentive.

'I go to QPR sometimes, and when you go to lower division games you get that "old school" feeling and atmosphere that our generation don't get in the top flight any more. There's passion, pride and you feel valued. Not in the Premiership you don't.'

By his own admission, Norman is luckier than most because he can afford to indulge what has become an expensive hobby, but he feels real anger for those disenfranchised by football's brave new commercial world.

'The clubs don't want the working man because there's not enough revenue to be squeezed out of him. They don't want his supposed "anti-social behaviour". They want to keep him at home, give him Sky TV, so that way they're still getting his money, cut down on their matchday costs and sell his seat to some corporate. I won't go in a box because of that, out of principle. The fans that want to come can't because of that. I've got a real issue with that.

'My kids got their first kits when they were babies, but for a kid today to support Spurs? It's a mockery – they might as well be wearing a Gillingham shirt.'

It is all a far cry from the 'Glory Days' when Norman first started following the club, in the late 1960s. 'I was an impressionable eight- or nine-year-old. I'm a Notting Hill boy, born and bred and QPR was my local club, but it was around the Cup final of 1967, Spurs playing Chelsea. Jimmy Greaves was my footballing hero after the World Cup of 1966, and even though the game was on TV in black and white, I remember that I just had an aversion to teams playing in blue.

'My first game was at QPR. I liked them, but I didn't get that spark, something didn't click. Same over at Chelsea, I didn't really like the atmosphere over there. I had family living in Edmonton and I was over there one weekend, and I saw all these fans walking towards White Hart Lane, loads of them, wearing blue and white scarves and I just thought, "This is it."

'I knew Tottenham was just down the road so I took a chance, sneaked out of the house and went down there on my own. I must have been about nine or ten. At that time it was just at the tail end of the era of "rattles", everyone seemed to smoke, everyone seemed to walk to the ground. I remember the smells of the fags, the hot dogs, the sight of the fans, the people selling rosettes and all the colour – it was just a hive of activity and I loved it. I was mesmerised by it all.

'Got in the ground and couldn't really see a thing and 'cos I was so tiny I got passed all the way to the front. I can't really remember the game; it was definitely a team in red, either Forest or Liverpool. Do you know what, that's gutted me ever since that I can't remember the game? I bought a programme and everything, to prove to the kids at school that I'd been to the game and I'm *sure* it was Liverpool. And that was it: I was hooked, absolutely hooked. Seeing players like Terry Venables, Cyril Knowles, Mike England and a young kid who came from my way, Steve Perryman, seeing them in the flesh, well . . .'

It probably would not happen in today's safety-conscious environment, but within a year of his first game Norman was a young child travelling up and down the country in support of his club. As a young black kid in an era when black faces were a rarity on the terraces, it was a doubly bold undertaking. It introduced Norman into a world where he felt a strong sense of comradeship and adventure that contradicts the orthodox image of football being a no-go area for young fans from ethnic minorities at the time.

'I went to as many home games as I could. I went to my first away game – again on my own. I sneaked off. It was at West Bromwich Albion. My old man used to work for the railways then and he used to have family tickets whereby we could get cheap travel. I saved all my dinner money up that week – I was starving – and bought a child return to Birmingham. I didn't know about football specials then and got an ordinary service train. I remember getting out at New Street, in the Bullring, and it was like being in another world. I'd never travelled that far before on my own.

'I was a bit intimidated and I didn't want to talk to anybody and I saw this black woman and I thought I'll go over to her and ask her how to get to West Bromwich. I couldn't understand a word she said. I couldn't believe it – she had a real strong Brummie accent. I just mumbled as if I understood, all I remembered was she said, "Get a number 27 bus and it will take you right outside the ground." She said, "It's in Smethwick", and I'm going, "No, no, West Bromwich." But I got on the bus and, true to her word, the bus stopped right outside the ground.

'It cost one shilling and sixpence to get in; I only had half a crown and enough for a Bovril. I hate Bovril, but I hadn't had anything to eat all day, and as long as I could get in that was all I was bothered about. I was in the West Brom end, so off came my scarf and rosette pretty sharpish. Spurs scored and suddenly I could see there were tons of Spurs behind me. I thought, "Great," and moved over to where they were and, "I'll stick with these." But the joy was short-lived – we lost 3–1. Tony "Bomber" Brown got a hat-trick for them.

'There were no other black kids at football then. I was the only black kid that used to go away with Tottenham and they treated me as a bit of a lucky mascot. Everyone knew me and sort of used to take care of me, no problems.'

So did Norman identify with black players? 'It meant a lot but then again it didn't. Maybe I was being naive, but I never thought of them as "black players", as long as they wore the shirt I didn't care what colour they were. To this day I still think that way. I only really saw the overt racism, chucking bananas at black players, etc., on the telly; I never saw that at Tottenham. So because you didn't experience it, it didn't really affect you. It went on, but maybe because London's a bigger, more cosmopolitan city, it was different. Even my black mates who were Chelsea, Millwall, West Ham fans, they never really experienced it.

'With Spurs I did feel a sense of belonging, otherwise I wouldn't have gone. I was always made to feel welcome, I was never made to feel "different", I can honestly say that.'

Even on the road Norman rarely felt threatened. A night job on the *Evening Post* provided the funds and the football specials the means to explore the whole country, largely in safety – though there was one particular incident that is still vivid in his memory.

'In all honesty, I hardly ever really experienced out and out racism. The hostility that I encountered was largely about me being a Spurs fan, being a "yid". Being a "black yid" just added to it: they hated you because you were a Tottenham fan first, not because you were black. The only time I really felt it, when it was right in front of my face, it was the year I left school, about '73–'74; we went to Liverpool away.

'We'd all heard stories – "Don't go up there, they hate blacks"; it was a common thing. You could go to the Midlands and not have any problems, but this was my first proper trip up north.

'We were on an ordinary train, about a hundred of us, and that's when I realised things weren't quite right. Normally, you go on a special with about six or seven hundred and when you got to the station there'd be police to escort you. Not this time. Got to Liverpool and there was what sounded like a million Scousers on the platform at Lime Street. Talk about a baptism of fire. I'll never forget that. I was with three of my black mates, a few white mates.

'There's all these Scousers sitting on that famous old wall at Lime Street (it's been knocked down now) where the buses used to come past and pick the fans up. Now my white mates had gone on and left us. And then we started to get it: "Hey, spook! Yer gonna fookin' die, nigger", and all the torrent of racial abuse was heavy. I'd never experienced anything like it in my life – they were spitting, everything.

'We fronted it out, tried to laugh it off, and we got on the bus. It kicked off proper, the first time we'd been really caught up in it. They got on the bus and pushed past our white mates to get to us. One of my mates – Charlie, we'll call him – kicked one of the Scousers down the stairs in self-defence and another one pulled a blade on us, a Stanley. By that time, all the other Tottenham fans on there had realised what was going on and rushed to help us. I can't remember quite what happened, but the last Scouser couldn't get down the stairs quick enough, so what he tried to do was get out of the escape window at the back.

'He's trying to climb out the back, traffic's stopped, there are bricks coming through the window, it's properly going off, we were shitting ourselves. The Scouser trying to get out of the window has dropped the blade and he's hanging by his fingertips on to the window from the top deck. A fella's gone "bosh" and hit his hands, he's fallen down and a car has hit him on the street below.

'The Scousers have all seen this and gone proper potty. Anyway, we get outside the ground, and it's gone mad, we're about to go in and we heard these shouts, "There's fookin' niggers", and they got us in the turnstile. We got slapped, one of my mates got cut. They weren't bothered about the white Tottenham fans – they were after us. We were only kids.'

It was a rude awakening to the painful reality that not all Liverpool fans were the wise-cracking, salt-of-the-earth types of popular myth.

'All that stuff about Liverpool fans and how wonderful they were, all of that was rubbish. Any football fan knew the truth. You'd have Jimmy Hill on *Match of the Day* going "those lovable Liverpool fans"; it was a nonsense. The worst racist fans I ever met were up there. I didn't go back for a few years. When I did go back, it was a cup game and we took 10,000 up there. We were a bit older and this time we were ready for anything.

'It never crossed my mind that I wouldn't go 'cos I'm black and it's not for me. I understand the football fan's psyche and I understood that they hated you for what you are as a fan. Being black was another reason to hate you because, as I subsequently found, I could go to any of those city centres in these places on any day but a matchday and those people would be perfectly fine to me, no problem. It's the football mentality.'

His awareness of that mentality meant a temporary parting of the ways between Norman Jay and football during the early 1980s, coinciding with the start of his career as a DJ.

'What made me decide to turn my back on football was Heysel. The terrace violence and the whole Casual thing was getting really naughty. It wasn't like the "good old days" of the 1970s where there'd be a mass bundle and no one really got hurt, no one really got nicked, just a £10 fine, Bow Street Magistrates' Court, you're laughing. People were getting properly hurt – it was nasty. I wasn't into that and I kind of knew a Heysel situation was going to happen. The Government weren't doing anything about it, neither were the Old Bill, and a lot of our lot were getting in serious trouble and I lost my appetite for it.

'Round that time I got involved in setting up Kiss FM. My first love was always music, with football a very, very close second. I was always a soul boy in the 1970s and there were a few clubs I'd always read about but could never go to. You couldn't stay there overnight. I was just a young schoolboy, but I remember what really fuelled it for me was the year Spurs got relegated.

'In the Second Division we had a game at Blackpool away and I thought, "Ah, great, I could go to the Blackpool Mecca," which was a big northern soul club. Keithy Robbins used to organise the coaches and we left the night before – horrible coach journey all the way up. We get there about six or seven in the morning the day of the match. Everyone can't wait for the boozers to open up on the front. Now I don't drink, so pubs meant nothing to me; I just thought the more you hang around in pubs, the more likely you were to get in bother.

'It's like Brighton, everyone went down the night before and the amount of running battles there used to be along the promenade, cor dear. Any seaside town, I didn't want any of that.

'I remember everyone was laughing at me 'cos I had a holdall with clothes to get changed into. I'd paid my return coach fare, but I had no intention of coming back after the game. The coach park and football ground was right next to the club and everyone's getting back on the coach about six or seven after the game. Keith goes to me, "Come on, we've been waiting for you." I said, "I'm not going back, I'm going to the club." He thought I was out of my mind, but three of us stayed and the coaches left. It's quite hard seeing half a dozen coaches leave and realising you are on your own.

'So, we had to keep a low one, away from the pubs, and we got changed in some beach-hut place. We joined the queue for the club and first of all they wouldn't let us in. We're going, "Come on, mate, we've come all the way up from London for this," but they were suspicious because they thought we were football fans. So we're going, "Nah, what, dressed like this? We're not football fans, we're into the cricket." That used to baffle them, it was always a good excuse, you used to say it to the Old Bill, "Nothing to do with us, mate, we're into the cricket." After a while, they let us in, and it was worth it as we had a top, top night in there.

'There were a few Spurs fans who were into it 'cos we were all soul boys. It was part of the youth culture – music, football, fashion, once you've got those three going on, that's it. We went to loads of these places: cities like Sheffield, Stoke, Wigan, the Casino, and all of these cities had clubs. Saturday was killing two birds with one stone.

'Spurs had a bit of a glamour, it was a bit of a London thing, but really it was undefinable. It was little things like having the cockerel on the badge. The football team I played in at the time, we wore all white and I put a cockerel on my shirt and a number eight on the back in tribute to Jimmy Greaves. I was quite a good footballer at that time. But the glamour was important – we were winning things, we played with a bit of flair.'

Oh for a bit of glamour and flair today. Where once the fans were just happy to be talking about the football, instead, they are forced to pick endlessly over the bones of season after season of underachievement and so-called 'transition'. Typically, for one so well versed in what the club should really be about, Norman has a perceptive take on what has gone wrong.

'It was round about the time of Sugar. We didn't move on; United were in a different league and they and Arsenal had a different overview of things. There was a ring of truth to what Sugar was saying about "Carlos Kickaballs", but you can't hold back the future.

'We were living off past glories too much, if you really want to know. Poor players, poor managers – even with the benefit of hindsight, I never thought Hoddle was the man. Players that played their football in the old First Division have got no real handle on how European football works, with the possible exception of two – Harry Redknapp and Sam Allardyce. They can manage teams.

'Hoddle is the man who turned down Okocha; who said that between Beckham and Redknapp, Redknapp had the bigger future. You're having a laugh! I always loved Hoddle as a player. I've been there when he's scored his great goals, real classics. But that doesn't make him a great manager. Look, I could have more records than anyone else, but that doesn't make me a great record producer. Hoddle's appointment was to appease the fans, who are blinded by an emotion that clouded the reality.

'The situation now is that Enic's hands are being forced. We're on a sound financial footing and we have to be. There's no point in having players on x-thousands of pounds a week if we can't afford it. It's only a matter of time before a Premiership club goes out of business, that's the reality. They will turn it around because they will have the financial clout to do so. Not doing a Leeds and spunking all the money, but given time they will do it.'

And of the remedies to right the many wrongs inflicted on the club and its fans? 'Of the current squad we should keep the kids. We need a Wenger-like Svengali figure who's English. My first instinct is not to go for a foreigner because he doesn't understand the ins and outs of Premiership, English football; a foreigner will only help you in Europe and we're not ready for Europe. We need to get the house in order, get the kids sorted, get the club back on track in a good old-fashioned way.

'Forget O'Neill – why would he want to take a backward step and join us? It's like me, playing in front of thousands of kids a week, suddenly playing in pubs round the corner in front of a handful of people. It's just not happening.

'We've got to show those managers that can work with nothing that we can give them a bit more money to work with. I mean, I might come across as a bit reactionary and right wing here, but what's the point in having a manager who the players will not be able to understand a word he's saying? Unless he's got charisma like Ranieri.

'You can always tell when the players don't like the manager. It was like that with Hoddle. They didn't want to play for him. We need a man-manager like Allardyce or Redknapp who get the best out of the kids. They don't talk about tactics and all that nonsense. They say to the kid, "You're good; this is what you need to do." Whether you're an East End boy like Redknapp or a hard northerner like Allardyce, they get the best out of those players. They're great; you keep them for a couple of years, and then when the team is ready for European football *then* you get in the Wenger-like European coach. We've got good kids, but no leaders; they just need good schooling.'

The unsavoury spectacle of seeing his club decline has left Norman with a degree of bitterness that most longstanding Tottenham supporters will empathise with. 'I've got mixed emotions because I will always defend the honour of the club, but when you analyse it, what are we defending? It's a misplaced passion, the club have never demonstrated a reciprocal passion to the fans, not in the modern era; we're just a cash cow to fuck for money.

'You go past that ground now when there's a game on and it's silent. When I was a kid, you'd come out of Seven Sisters and you knew something big was going on. There was an excitement that we only had against Arsenal – and even that was an excitement based on rage.

'The problem is that the fans are so justifiably frustrated they won't give Enic the time, and why should we? If they'd have shown some goodwill to the supporters, giving a little bit back for what we had given them, showing a little bit of generosity, we'd be more patient; we'd be like Pompey fans. But there ain't goodwill to the team because you don't get value for money and we don't *feel* valued.'

Norman has personal experience of how supporter loyalty has not been repaid. 'A couple of years ago we were playing Leeds. I took my two boys and a nephew. I promised them a day out – we'd all been looking forward to it; it means a lot to me as well to take them. We get to the end of Park Lane by the High Road and there's a big line of police and I thought, there's been some trouble here. We were going past the police to get in and one of them puts his hand on me. He said, "Are you a member?" I said, "What? Don't talk to me about being a member, I've been coming to this ground for God knows how long, so don't give me that." But he wouldn't let us through, "Members or season-ticket holders only through here."

'I went in the club shop and asked what all this nonsense was, as it was the start of the time when they stopped you paying on the day. All the time and money you've spent, all the loyalty you've given them and they wouldn't let us in. I was gutted for the kids and I thought, "Fuck you, Tottenham, I ain't gonna come in here again." But you know what it's like, it's an emotional thing.

'So I thought, "Right, we'll do it rationally, we'll make all the kids members," only to find the membership scheme is a con – it didn't guarantee you a ticket. What's all that about? So I refused to buy the Tottenham shirt, I went through a whole anti-club thing. Deep down, I supported them, but I really resented the whole commercial aspect, and you could see everyone was feeling the same. It's what fuels the angst among fans – they're ripped off, so they're less tolerant.'

That lack of patience and tolerance extends to the players. 'I don't want to know them or be cosy with them, so I can sit there on a

Saturday (or a Sunday) and say, "You're a wanker." I knew a few players – Sol Campbell, Tim Sherwood a little bit . . . I've done a few social things with them, but I don't really want to have much to do with them. They are professionals doing a job.'

Norman had to adopt much the same attitude when he was called upon to do what must rank as one of his most testing gigs, the story of which has become the subject of much legend among fans on both sides of the north London divide. Now, he can reveal the truth.

'I did Thierry Henry's wedding,' Norman admits, making it sound like a confession. 'I didn't want to, but I didn't really know it was him. The story is my management got a call from one of the biggest high-brow party organisers. They arrange dos for the stars and wanted a high-profile DJ for an "A-list celeb. We won't tell you who until you sign a confidentiality clause." So I asked my manager, Dan, and he didn't know who it was. It went backwards and forwards. My view was, I don't need to do this, I don't care. Eventually they let on that it's a footballer, but they still want this confidentiality clause. I maintained that I won't do it till I know who it is.

'After a few weeks, they got back, they must have really wanted me to do it and they kept on upping the money. Finally, Dan finds out who it is and it's Henry. I've met him a couple of times, got on well with him and I said, "I'll do it; if it was any other Gooner I wouldn't but I'll do it for him." And I said to Dan, "Look, I am the biggest Tottenham fan you can imagine, and I'm being asked to DJ for the number one top Gooner in the world – I don't need a confidentiality clause, there's no way in the world I'm going to be talking about this one! But no friends or favours on the door for this one, no way, they pay!"

'It was a castle down in Hampshire, very posh, no expense spared, a civilised affair, low key, close family and friends, only about 60 people. I wore the tiniest cockerel badge: I had to make a stand of some kind. The players who were there came over, shook my hand, said they're enjoying the music, and it was [Patrick] Vieira who spotted it. He pointed at the badge and started laughing, so at least he's got a sense of humour.

'Everyone asked, "Would you have done it if Sol Campbell had been there?" He wasn't about by then. Some people said I was like Campbell being a Judas for doing it!

'My view of him is that my emotional side, like everyone else, thinks he was a tosser for joining them; the professional side of me says he had to do what he had to do. You have to separate the two. If my son was going to be a professional footballer and Arsenal came in for him tomorrow, would I let him join? Of course I would. It's about a professional doing a job, and that part of it I understood. Anyone who put the club first would have been a fool, it had to be an unemotional, rational decision. And he's been proved right – look at what he's done. It hurts, what happened, but it's time we all moved on.'

Time is moving on. Norman has got to go to another meeting and prepare for his radio show. He's a man in demand; throughout the interview he's been bombarded with greetings, requests upon his time and expertise and the odd mickey-take from passing Arsenal fans and fellow DJs. He speaks with a degree of sadness about how many members of his profession are Gooners. 'There's still a few Spurs, though – Brandon Block, Alex P, Paul "Trouble" Anderson, though he doesn't really go. Pete Heller does, though – he's a big Tottenham fan.'

Perhaps tired of all the justifiable complaints, he reflects for a moment on when things were far better for Tottenham supporters – and try as he might, that unmistakable enthusiasm of the die-hard fan comes to the fore. 'I've seen some great games, great games. In the old First Division when we won 9–0, Colin Lee scored four; Wembley '81, unbelievable; Southampton away when we got promoted, millions of Spurs down there. All the cup games, the semi at Hillsborough when Hoddle scored an unbelievable goal. The replay when we filled the North Bank, we ran on the pitch at Highbury, 3–0, magic. Hoddle was a great player. Crooks, Archibald. But it's people like Chivers, Gilzean, Pat Jennings, Greavsie, people from that first era when I started to go, who I like most.

'I'll still go; that's it once you're in, you're in for life. I used to organise my gigs around games, I'd drive all over the country. I did a gig in Cornwall once and went all the way up to Newcastle to see us get beat 7–1. I come back and I think, "No way." But I still have the passion. Not as strong as it was, because we're getting nothing back. But who'd want to be a manager, or who'd want to be a club director?' Norman says, smiling.

16

We'll support you ever more:
Ella Davies Oliveck

Tottenham Hotspur
Tottenham Hotspur
We'll support you ever more

The point snatched from Arsenal had not quite made Spurs safe, but events away from their next game did so. On the following Saturday, Leicester and Wolves were relegated and, when news that Leeds United's defeat at Bolton had effectively demoted the Yorkshire side came through at half-time during Tottenham's Sunday game at Aston Villa, Spurs knew they were safe.

It was just as well, as yet another insipid performance saw Tottenham lose without scoring a goal. 'Spurs play as individuals, not as a team,' observed Russell Kempson in *The Times*, before going on to make a telling observation. When Spurs had beaten Villa 2–1 at White Hart Lane in November, the Midlanders were in 18th place while Spurs looked to be on the up. In the 23 games since, Villa had won 44 points and were now an outside bet for the final Champions League spot. Spurs, meanwhile, had picked up only 24 points and were on course for their worst-ever finish in the Premiership.

Relief of a sort came with the final home game of the season against Blackburn, as Spurs at last recorded a win – the first in nine games. The game provided a microcosm of the season. First, there was a stunning winning goal from Jermain Defoe, and then, veering from the sublime to the ridiculous, Anthony Gardner gave his now familiar rendition of simultaneous class and circus act (which had reportedly given Chris Hughton nightmares). There was also a supporter protest (of sorts), with half the capacity crowd singing 'Stand up, if you want Pleat out.'

The chairman, Daniel Levy, seemed to echo their thoughts, referring in his programme notes to the 'appalling' end to the season, assuring readers that he would make the 'difficult' but necessary changes – but absolving himself of any blame.

There was no mistaking who Levy had in his sights. David Pleat was an increasingly isolated figure, weighed down by his own errors while being forced to shoulder the mistakes of others. Even his sternest critics had to warm to his comic timing, however, when Pleat sprang from his seat in the dugout just as the song calling for his head got into full swing.

But by far the most notable feature of the day was the extraordinary spectacle of the vast majority of the fans staying behind for the team's traditional lap of honour. As websites and message boards noted, it was a stunning example of the loyalty of Tottenham supporters, in stark contrast to the so-called 'best fans in the world' at Newcastle, who booed their team off a day later.

Perhaps the sight of Ricky Villa at half-time had put the Spurs fans in a generous mood. To complete an odd week, there was an admission from some players that they should shoulder part of the blame for the club's poor campaign. While Freddie Kanouté professed himself unable to explain the loss of form (forgetting his own African sojourn), Jamie Redknapp and Dean Richards admitted that the players had to acknowledge their part.

A 2–0 victory at relegated Wolves meant Spurs finished on 45 points in 14th place, thereby maintaining the unenviable record of never having finished in the top or bottom six places of the Premiership. Spurs were a comfortable 12 points above the drop zone, but this disguised the narrowness of their top-flight survival.

Redknapp, meanwhile, had been granted a one-year extension to his deal, despite other injury-prone and past-their-sell-by-date players Gus Poyet, Christian Ziege and Darren Anderton getting their P45s. Paul Robinson finally completed his move to Spurs a day later, but there was really only one new recruit the supporters were interested in. And eight months on, they were still waiting for The Man, as they had been for years.

Still waiting, and still watching, as Arsenal completed a whole season unbeaten, as former poor relations Chelsea finished runners-up, and as Manchester United fans rued 'only' finishing third.

For any impressionable young football fan, the temptations of these three teams are obvious. It can seem that today's generation of child football fans are more interested in following the team that is successful, or on the television the most, rather than the club of their family or local heritage.

So imagine you are a young child, living in Finsbury Park, right in the heart of Arsenal country. Step out of your front door and you can almost hear the murmur of polite applause wafting over from Highbury as Thierry Henry rattles in yet another goal. Most of the kids at your school support Arsenal; of the ones that don't the majority support Manchester United and the rest are flirting with the idea of following Chelsea. Well, would you support Tottenham?

Ella Davies Oliveck does. At just seven years old, Ella is already a fully fledged fan with several home games under her belt. She knows the players, the songs, loves White Hart Lane and already has a clear idea of what it means to be a football fan. And she definitely does not want to support Arsenal.

'At my school there are only one or two of them who support Spurs, a boy and a girl. The rest of them support Arsenal. And Chelsea and Manchester United. Some of them tease me. One girl says "Arsenal" and I say "Tottenham!" I said one boy had chicken legs and he was a loser because he supported Arsenal.

'Sometimes I go with my daddy, sometimes my mummy and sometimes my little brother, Isaac.'

Mummy and Daddy are Melissa Oliveck and Steve Davies, both longstanding contributors to the Spurs fanzine *Cock-a-Doodle Doo* and prominent in the early days of supporters' groups. Steve was once active to such an extent that Terry Venables suggested a place for him on the board during the former manager's power struggle with Alan Sugar.

Both parents made certain that Ella was recruited to the Spurs cause as soon as possible. She went to Wimbledon away a week before she was born and made her actual debut at a game against Coventry a few months later. Since then, she has developed clear ideas as to what she enjoys about being a fan.

'I like watching the players. My favourite is Robbie Keane, he's good at scoring goals, and Jamie Redknapp. He's the captain. I support Ireland as well, because Robbie Keane comes from Ireland.'

The matchday experience revolves around getting kitted out in her Spurs shirt, hat and scarf, the culinary delights of a White Hart Lane burger, sweets, Chirpy the mascot and, best of all, celebrating the all too rare spectacle of a home goal. Four-year-old Isaac interjects in praise of standing up and cheering, which reminds Ella to point out that 'playing with the seats' also counts high in a young fan's list of priorities.

Even at such a tender age, Ella has become a vocal supporter, announcing 'I sing "Come on you Spurs"', before giving a word-perfect rendition of the 'Postiga' song. 'She's very good at that,' says Mum. 'She sings virtually all the way through the game.' Ella is also acutely aware of the various rituals that have to be observed. Once, she mentioned to her dad at half-time, 'If I wasn't here, you'd be using the "f" word, wouldn't you, Daddy?'

Ella's emerging love for the game extends to playing it, modelling herself, naturally, on Robbie Keane. She plays at school and has been training at some of the coaching schools organised by Spurs. At the first session she went to, Ella was not just the only girl there but also the youngest, at just six. Despite 'the boys saying rude things to me', Ella persevered and continues to take part in the training days.

For attending one session she was rewarded with tickets for a home game – perhaps a sign of a good bit of Spurs PR, for a change? That is only half the story. A glaring example of how Spurs have lagged behind in the campaign to win hearts and minds is that the club does not run such a 'soccer school' in Ella's home borough of Hackney. Once – and to an extent still – one of the main areas of Spurs support, the borough is now obviously viewed by Spurs as not worthwhile for attracting young fans. Instead, the schools are largely held in the suburbs or home-counties towns like Broxbourne.

'I rang Spurs up once,' says Melissa, 'and asked the club why. They said that they do free coaching at schools in Haringey, but I pointed out there was not one in Hackney, where there are kids who do support Spurs and do want to go to the training sessions. Their response? They said, "We'll look into it."'

Surrounded by young Arsenal fans when she plays at another training club run for kids on Highbury Fields, Ella still proudly wears her Spurs shirt. Anything Tottenham-related, in fact, gets her approval; she was a willing volunteer taster when Spurs launched their own branded ice cream and is a keen member of Junior Spurs, hoping against hope to be a mascot for a game. She also is the proud owner of an autograph book bearing the names of players, some of which she has queued up for for three hours.

Dad arrives home from work, bearing tickets for Ella's first-ever away game – a trip to Wolves for the last match of the season. Ella swiftly notices the old-gold livery of the tickets and you can see her eyes light up. It's that sense of anticipation common to all fans – even in a day and age when following Tottenham has been less a privilege and more a test of endurance.

Ella missed the Arsenal home game: duty called at a friend's birthday party. Even so, in a bold challenge to the overwhelming Arsenal support in her area (and with a show of spirit too many of the Spurs players had failed to provide throughout the season), Ella nailed her Spurs colours metaphorically to the mast. 'I put up things in the window saying, "Come on you Spurs" and saying "Boo Arsenal",' she says, proudly. 'We don't put anything up too noticeable so we get a brick through the window, but just a small sign of defiance,' says Steve. Ella even wore her Spurs scarf to school the next day.

All her extended family are Spurs fans, as are her elder sister Poppy (14) and elder brother Callum (11), and she was told that if she should start to support Arsenal, 'I'll be kicked out of the house, into the garden. But I could climb over the fence.' Such football fundamentalism has clearly had its effect: 'My auntie has had a baby called Tyler and I'm going to teach him to be a Spurs fan. If he's not, I'll throw him to the crocodiles.' And, with the enthusiasm, confidence and sheer hope typical not just of seven-year-olds, but football fans of all ages, she is already looking forward to season 2004–05. 'I think we'll play better,' she says.

Her enthusiasm is infectious. 'She is very vocal, she's always cheering Spurs on,' says Steve. 'It's a good experience for a parent; it's an antidote to all the cynicism. Isaac's got it sussed, though, he shouts out, "Come on you Spurs, for God's sake."' Ella quickly reminds Steve of her own positive attitude. 'Once, I shouted, "Come on you Spurs", and a man in the seats above us shouted out, "That's my girl!"'

We all laugh. At the end of a miserable season, humour is a commodity that has been in short supply when it comes to Tottenham. When enthusiasm and optimism have been lacking, it is fans like Ella, the new generation, that give cause for hope.

We Are Tottenham

Because, despite all the frustration, the despair, the cynicism and the anger, and the overwhelming sense of being let down, the fans – the loyal, vocal fans – are still there. All kinds of people from all kinds of backgrounds, races and creeds, from the youngest to the oldest, are all still defiantly proud to say, 'We are Tottenham.'

Epilogue

You wait nine months for a Messiah to come along and look what happens – three arrive at once. After enduring a season of huge disappointment, Tottenham fans at last had something to smile about when chairman Daniel Levy pulled several rabbits out of the hat.

With the 2003–04 season barely ended, Levy made his first decisive move by dismissing Director of Football David Pleat. Dignified words were exchanged by both parties at the parting of the ways, but the message from the board was clear: out with the old, in with the new.

The new was a surprise: Frank Arnesen, a former Denmark international who had forged a highly successful career in Holland as a coach, scout and technical director, most notably at PSV Eindhoven. Arnesen was not a name that had featured high on the list of Tottenham's prospective new leaders, but his appointment represented a significant step forward.

He arrived with a glowing CV for spotting and nurturing talent (Ronaldo and Ruud van Nistelrooy included) and was installed as 'Sporting Director' – not just a new label for Pleat's old job but a more clearly defined role than that 'enjoyed' by his predecessor. Arnesen was to be a non-executive director, but one with responsibility for general football management including, crucially, the final say on transfers.

It was still the position of manager – or rather head coach under Levy's bright and shiny new management structure – that the fans were really interested in, however. June arrived with no clear candidate and a growing sense of unease among the faithful. Matters took a confusing turn when Levy and his co-director Paul Kemsley were spotted at Heathrow in conversation with the recently deposed Chelsea boss Claudio Ranieri and his representatives; a double-page feature on the story appeared in the *Evening Standard*, complete with snatched pictures of the Spurs directors and an unconvincing assertion from Levy that the meeting was merely a 'coincidence'.

Scorn was once more heaped on Spurs for their apparent bumbling. But, it was the chairman who had the last laugh. For, just two days later, the big one was announced: Jacques Santini, the incumbent manager of the French national side was to be the new Tottenham boss.

This was big news, propelling Spurs into the sporting limelight not just in Britain but across the Continent. Media reaction was mixed: for every hack applauding Levy for his most audacious appointment yet, journalists of a more hostile persuasion were incredulous about why one of the world's top coaches should decide to move to White Hart Lane. They were led by Patrick Collins in the *Mail on Sunday*, whose spiteful article on Santini's appointment was an anti-Spurs rant par excellence.

Away from the bluster and bias, the truth, probably, was that a series of happy circumstances had fallen neatly into place. By the club's official admission, the original target had been Trappatoni, but the deal had fallen through. Denying that any others had been approached, the club insisted that Santini was the only other real candidate.

Given that Santini confirmed that his interest was sparked by an approach from Arnesen, and the French boss admitted he had only opted for Spurs due to the French FA's reluctance to offer him a new contract, it seemed clear that his arrival was not the result of the seamless, defined strategy that Levy wanted people to believe he was following. But the doubters were given a perfect riposte when another highly regarded Continental coach, Martin Jol, was appointed as Santini's deputy, the managerial transformation was complete, and whether by accident or design, Levy had delivered.

For the first time in months, Spurs fans were confident about the future, even if this confidence was tempered by the experience of so many false dawns. The root and branch change that, deep down, many had known was needed looked set to happen, and the nature of Tottenham Hotspur at the beginning of the new season would be very different to the wounded beast that had finished the old. Finally, it felt good to be a Spurs fan again.